Through My Garden Gate

Leah Friedman

Leah Friedman

Through My Garden Gate
By Leah Friedman

Copyright © 2021 by Leah Friedman

All rights reserved.
Printed in the United States of America.

ISBN: 978-0-578-88662-6

Cover photograph by Leah Friedman.

Author photograph by Harriet Blickenstaff.

Cover and interior design by Magdaline Middeke.

My garden is a sanctuary,
a haven, and a place of beauty.
It offers a way to connect with
nature, provides security,
and gives me a feeling
of comfort and peace.

Table of Contents

Prologue
The Hidden Flower

Nature and Nurture 1
Flowers 3
Trees 8
The Autumnal Equinox 12
Love 16
Soup 22
Homes 25
Wild, Warm, and Wonderful 36

Connecting 43
Writing 45
Our Salon 49
Unlikely Friends 52
Relationships 56
Up-LYFT-ting 63
Support 66
Kindness 69

Table of Contents continued

The Self 73
Identity 75
An Alternative Self 79
Chapters 83
The Essential Self 89
A Theme Revisited 96
The Stories We Tell Ourselves 102
Daily Challenges 107
Observing, Discerning, Judging 110
Generosity 114

Aging 119
Newly Ninety 121
Aging and Attitude 123
Letting Go 129
Relevance and Irrelevance 134
Lacunae 138
Coping with Hearing Loss 142
The Loss of Desire 146
Becoming a Sage 150

Death	157
The Squirrel	159
The Hawk	161
Regrets	163
A Funeral and Lessons Learned	170
Do I Matter?	174
Harvesting	178
A Good Death	181
Disruption	185
Dealing with Covid-19	187
Transformation	195
Living with Uncertainty	198
Reciprocity	205
Ennui and Angst	209
Our Unfinished Nation	214
Epilogue	219
Enduring and Evolving	221
Acknowledgements	225

Prologue

My garden is a sanctuary where I come to reflect on my life's journey. It provides me with a refuge from the stresses and strains of everyday life, a welcome respite in these chaotic times. It is a place of beauty and calm where tumult recedes and tranquility reigns. When I am in my garden, I am filled with a sense of gratitude, wellbeing, and security. This small, brick-enclosed space adjoins a convenient parking lot, so my friends can enter through my garden gate, making our visits safe from fear of Covid-19, the scourge of our time.

These reflections are drawn from the most recent three years of my journey, almost all written since my 90th birthday. But my interest in contemplation, a desire to explore my inner-most self, and a need to grow in insight and understanding, reach back many years. So I begin this book of reflections with *The Hidden Flower*, a recently uncovered essay I wrote more than twenty years ago.

As the friends and family I cherish push open and walk through my garden gate, I invite them to leave the outer world behind and join me in my lovely, peaceful garden. As they cross the threshold, they also enter into my welcoming, loving heart. May these reflections grant the same warm reception to all who enter this metaphorical garden of shared memories and hopes.

Leah Friedman

The Hidden Flower

What is this presence within my chest that pushes against my sternum, reaching for release with each cycle of breath? What is it that feels heavy, pregnant with desire to be free? What is it that longs to come alive, to lift its face to the sun, to bask in the glow of respect and love? What lies within my heart that is unexpressed, unseen, unacknowledged? Some unarticulated, barely recognized, yet palpable yearning demands my attention.

Recently an image of that longing came to me: a flower wishing and needing to burst forth into its full and bountiful blossoming beauty. That barely formed, unidentified flower is now hidden in dark shadows, a tightly furled bud that long ago became discouraged in its effort to unfold into full flowering. It is stunted, pale, under-fertilized, poorly rooted, lacking in sturdy branching and leafing. It hungers for nourishment, thirsts for recognition of its potential beauty and worthiness, and reaches for the light of liberation.

When I recently participated in a meditation on the heart, which involved imagining being *within* my own heart, my most strongly felt sensations were of heat and moisture. Those are the conditions requisite for growth, for seeds to germinate, and for flowers to bloom. It would seem, based on this imaginary journey inward, that the proper environment already exists, that the necessary circumstances for the nurturance and feeding of this veiled flower are readily available, but have not been utilized. Perhaps it is time to feed the flower of my soul, to allow it to explode in all its dazzling, glorious, majestic splendor. Perhaps it is time to celebrate my own inner beauty, my own soul's goodness, intelligence, and maturity.

Yes, perhaps it is time, but even as I write those words, doubts arise. How can I say that I possess beauty, majesty, goodness, intelligence? Those descriptive terms immediately ring false, feel undeserved, sound boastful and unbecoming. Robert Sardello, in a recent lecture, referred to this reaction as the "agnostic reflex," defined as the doubt that arises about our own imaginative efforts. He recommends that we not deny that doubt, but look on it as a helper. He rightly says that doubt is more clever than we will ever be, that we cannot deny it, or banish it. However, we can use doubt to our advantage if we are willing to dialogue with it, listen to it, and learn from it. It can help us be more discerning, more accurate, more certain of the true nature of our imaginative efforts. It can help us become more confident and more trusting of our own creative imagination.

So, now to dialogue with my own doubt about my flowering, which at the moment feels more like a shrinking violet than the expansive, fragrant, full-blossomed flower that I had hoped to envision. Who speaks so disparagingly? Who says I can never be the tallest poppy or the most beautiful rose or the sunniest sunflower? What is so terrible about being the best one can be? Why is fulfilling one's inner potential something shameful? How do I counter the negative voice of my own agnostic reflex?

The voice of doubt within me is, of course, that of my introjected negative mother, she who disapproves, who withholds, who judges, who scolds, who finds no joy in life. Since she has little pleasure of her own, she wishes to deny me my full measure. She is jealous of my childhood exuberance, of my freedom, of my talents, of my budding beauty, and most especially of my closeness to my Dad.

Well, that description is of my outer mother, certainly, but how about the voice of the inner mother? What does she have to say? She says I am not *enough*: not smart enough, not good enough, not generous enough, not pretty enough, not compassionate enough, not understanding enough, not talented enough—and on and on. She has a long list of not-enoughs, ready for any occasion that might arise. These are the attitudes that have spoiled my successes, that have denigrated my abilities, that have diminished my accomplishments, and that have inhibited the growth of my inner flower.

How may I enter into a meaningful and beneficial relationship with this demeaning and dismissive figure? How can I translate this negativity into something positive and nurturing? How can I transform these rotten beliefs into rich, nutritious compost that will fertilize the flower of my soul? What seems to be called for is an alchemical process: *nigredo*, meaning to decay, putrefy, dissolve, disintegrate into the primordial essence, to become *prima materia*, potentiality itself. Then, by entering into that pit of empty fullness, that place of luminous fruitful darkness, I may discover the fructifying promise that will reconstitute my being, like the caterpillar dissolving and then restructuring itself into the butterfly.

Such a process may provide a deeper rootedness and a richer sustenance, allowing my aching closeted essence to erupt into its full measure of glorious beauty, satisfying its need to be a full-fledged blooming explosion of color, fragrance, and form.

Nature and Nurture

SEPTEMBER 2018

Flowers

Nature provides us with many pleasures, but perhaps none is so overwhelmingly delightful to the eyes and heart as the sight of beautiful, blooming plants. The flowering plants offer their blossoms freely, giving us their beauty and their fragrance with no expectation of anything in return. While true that they also attract butterflies and bees that help pollinate other plants, it is their feast for the eyes that captivates me. Perhaps it is because I value my small garden so very much, that I have begun to think about the place that flowers have played in my personal history.

I have few enjoyable memories of my childhood on the farm in North Carolina where I was raised. But one thing I recall with pleasure is my mother's flower garden. It was enclosed within a wire fence with a white wooden gate through which one entered. Straight ahead was a small pond, filled with goldfish and a few water-friendly plants. To the left was an arbor with painted white benches, over which climbed red-flowered honeysuckle. The arbor, where as a child I liked to play with my dolls, was a lovely addition to the garden which was chockfull of flowers. I wish I could remember all their names, but only a few come to mind: hollyhocks, feverfew, petunias, iris, foxgloves, larkspur, and pansies. Lots of pansies, which in North Carolina wintered over.

The pansies are especially meaningful to me, for one of my pleasant childhood memories is that I often gathered bunches of colorful pansies to take to my teachers. In many ways these women (of course in those days, all were women, and almost all unmarried), were life-savers for me, offering me the kind of attention, stimulation, and encouragement that I did not get at home. The gift of flowers—plus being a good and enthusiastic student—was my way of showing them my gratitude for their kindness.

When I returned to the South for my mother's funeral (she lived to age 93), I stayed with a cousin who also had pansies in her garden. I asked if I could pick a few, and just as my mother's casket was being lowered into the ground, I placed a fistful of pansies on top, a final remembrance of something positive in what had been a troubled, sometimes acrimonious, relationship.

In the 1980s I became friends with a young woman who taught Ikebana, the Japanese art of flower arrangement. There are over 1,000 different schools of this centuries-old art, and I do not recall the name of the one she followed. But I came to greatly appreciate the careful, contemplative approach to flower arranging that characterizes Ikebana. For a while my daughter and granddaughter joined me in my lessons. I began making arrangements and though I no longer follow the prescribed rules, I still find joy in having a vase or two of cut flowers in my home.

During the time of those lessons I got to know two men who owned a flower shop near my home. They were talented arrangers themselves and always had a large variety of both common and exotic flowers plus what is called "line material," that is, greenery or other filler plant items to help give movement and/or substance to arrangements. These men became my friends and were generous and indulgent in that they allowed me to go into the cooler in which they kept their flowers. I could choose anything I wanted. It was magical. I grieved the loss when they sold their shop and moved out of town. Now I can get flowers in grocery stores, but I miss the joy of entering that cooler and choosing from the vast array of blooms and other plant material available there.

When I began to travel to California once a month for my graduate studies in 1997, I discovered in Carpinteria, where Pacifica Graduate Institute was located, a street vendor whose stand had a wonderful assortment of fresh flowers. The woman who ran it was gifted in putting together lovely, colorful arrangements for very little money. So, after driving up the coast from the Los Angeles airport, my first stop was at her stall where I bought a vase of flowers to place in my motel room. The room itself was rather drab, but it contained a low chest with a large mirror behind it. Each time over the three years I traveled there I spread out a cloth and arranged a small altar with some photos and other items I brought from home. But the centerpiece was always the vase of flowers. It transformed that dreary, ordinary space into something welcoming and more home-like.

Some time ago, as I began thinking about the celebration of my ninetieth birthday, my first thought was that I wanted to have lots of flowers. Accordingly, I bought pots of blooming plants for the entrance to my condo and also ones for the entrance hall and hearth. I made an arrangement for the buffet and placed small vases of lovely multi-hued roses on the dining room table. My granddaughter Jessie, who assembled a sumptuous altar with items of remembrance from all my family members, added a generous selection of beautiful flowers. So I was not only surrounded by those I love most, who expressed their love in multitudinous ways, but was also enveloped by the beauty of flowers. I could not have asked for more.

In the various homes in which I have lived, I have almost always had gardens or potted plants. But none were so fulfilling as the one I have now in my old age. Each morning, weather permitting, I walk outside and say "Thank you" to the plants and flowers in my garden. I marvel at the towering, magnificent river birch that provides dappled shade, and admire the dogwood tree that reaches out its horizontal limbs as if offering itself to the world. I express my appreciation for the herbs, which give me seasonings for my food, for the begonias and impatiens that add color, the exuberant coleus plants that have grown tall and luxurious, the liriope, pachysandra, ferns, and wild ginger that add texture, the astonishing variety of hostas which enjoy the shade provided by the birch. I am thankful for the potted palm whose massive fronds lean gracefully and protectively over the bench on which I love to sit. And, of course, I am grateful for the little pond with its burbling sound as the water flows over the rocks, where my great-grandchildren now have fun splashing around just as their mothers did a generation ago. In these later years of my life I have the great joy, at least in the milder months, of sitting outside taking in the beauty of the plants and flowers. I cannot fully convey my indebtedness to my garden for the soul nourishment it so unstintingly provides.

My friend Sara, an art historian (as well as the editor of my previous books), recently told me about the concept of *hortus conclusus*, a Latin term meaning "enclosed garden." She said that in medieval art such a garden was symbolic of the virginity of Mary, representing her "closed off" womb, protected from sin by a wall. My small garden is enclosed by brick walls on the sides and a fence covered with Boston ivy at the rear. And though I am certain it has not protected me from sin (whatever that may be), the enclosure provides a place of safety, serenity, and privacy.

As a final thought, I have written about my wish to have a natural, green burial, with no chemicals involved—just wrapped in a white linen shroud and placed into the earth. However, I feel certain that my loved ones will see to it that my shroud is covered with blossoms, so I can enter the great mysterious beyond knowing that my love of flowers has been remembered and honored.

APRIL 2019

Trees

At one time I kept a journal, sporadically, and have several notebooks filled with feelings, thoughts, and dreams from earlier in my life. Recently I looked at a few of them and found some of my musings so painful that I destroyed quite a few pages. I did not wish to inflict those sad, despairing memories on anyone. However, today I looked at another journal and found an entry I would like to share with you. It was written in June 1991, in our Lakewood Hills home where I had gone alone for the weekend. This is what I wrote:

Being in Lakewood Hills calms me, gives me a sense of peace and well-being. Tonight, as I look out at the trees, I am struck by the qualities these wonderful "beings" have, and feel reverence in their presence. I desire to develop in my own life some of the qualities that I see in these trees surrounding our home.

Stillness. *It is twilight. The trees are quiet, resting, although there is much activity—birds nesting, squirrels running, frogs and insects preparing for the night. Stillness in the midst of activity.*

Strength. *Trees appear rigid with solid trunks, but they are also capable of flexibility—bending with the wind, sending roots down deep for moisture and nutrients.*

Dignity. *Trees are reserved, undemanding, noble; they call for our respect.*

Protection. *In a calm and unpretentious way, the trees provide cover, shelter, and shade for a great variety of life forms.*

Wisdom. *Somehow I feel that the trees, the large stately ones, have accumulated great wisdom through years of patient growth and maturation.*

Beauty. *Whether in the delicacy of spring, the lush fullness of summer, the blazing colors of autumn, or the sharp angularity of winter, they always display a majestic beauty.*

Endurance. *Through storms, droughts, floods, deprivations, the trees continue to stand, indomitable, steady, reliable.*

Aspiration. *While rooted solidly in the earth—in everyday reality—trees also reach for the skies, for light, for sustenance, and for guidance.*

I greatly appreciate the convenience and comfort of currently living in an urban setting, but this journal entry reminds me of something lost by not being as close to nature. When we lived in that house nestled among the trees it is pleasing to know that I appreciated what the trees had to offer. I can now affirm and perhaps expand on what each of those qualities has meant to me in the years since I was so moved by the trees.

I really like that word *stillness*, a quality which implies mindfulness, being present in the moment. It suggests the ability to remain centered and calm in the midst of chaos, a quality especially needed in our current era of divisiveness and crudeness. I associate stillness with solitude, the capacity to stand quietly and assuredly alone, even in a crowd.

Strength, both inner and outer, is something we all need as we are faced with life's certain misadventures, loss, illness, and failure. Trees have sturdy trunks with roots deep enough to withstand heavy winds. For us it is a strong core that is rooted in fundamental ethics and morality but which has the necessary resilience to adjust when our circumstances change—as they inevitably will.

We all admire persons who carry themselves with *dignity*, whose demeanor reveals a measure of confidence and self-respect. This kind of dignity often requires a level of maturity and stability, of being firmly planted in a comfortable sense of self, a stateliness and authenticity that comes of having lived a full and considered life.

If we are fortunate enough, as I am, to have a family of children, grandchildren, and great-grandchildren, then it is easy to understand the need to provide *protection* for those we love. We wish to keep them safe from danger, physical or emotional. But we must be careful that our protectiveness does not thwart growth. Just as most plants do not thrive under too much shade, our children are best served if given the opportunity to move beyond the hovering branches of overprotective parents.

Who does not admire *wisdom*? Wisdom is difficult to define, but some of the qualities are authenticity, patience, compassion, kindness, humility, humor, playfulness, confidence, acceptance, awareness, serenity, and optimism. By applying and integrating as many of these traits as possible throughout our lives, we can become carriers of wisdom, a gift to those who come after us.

Just as trees have different kinds of *beauty* depending on the seasons, so it is with us humans. In my late years, I can now appreciate the many manifestations of beauty I see around me—the joyfulness of children, the emerging selfhood of adolescents, the vigor of young adults, the maturity of middle-aged adults, and the very special, fragile beauty of the old. If we look beyond the surface we can find something pleasing to the eye regardless of stage of life.

If we live long enough, we have proved the value of *endurance*. We have survived the trials and sorrows that life has given us to withstand, be it illness, divorce, or the death of family members and friends. We have benefited not only from having endured but also from having overcome the many obstacles. We have learned to persevere in order to continue to grow and learn.

And finally, *aspiration*. It is interesting that I included this one in my journal, for I don't think it would ordinarily be considered a characteristic of trees. But it seems entirely appropriate. Perhaps all living entities have some form of reaching for betterment or fulfillment in whatever milieu they find themselves. I certainly find it true of myself in my old age as I continually aspire to live a life of gratification, meaningfulness, and tranquility.

Though I no longer live among the trees, I am fortunate to have a magnificent river birch and a lovely dogwood in my small garden. So I shall use this reflection as a reminder to review the many lessons to be learned by observing the majesty of my trees and others in my neighborhood. The qualities I observed then seem as essential today as they were 28 years ago.

SEPTEMBER 2018

The Autumnal Equinox

Today, Saturday, September 22, 2018, at 8:54 pm, marks the official autumnal equinox in St. Louis. The spring and fall equinoxes are the moments the sun crosses the celestial equator – the imaginary line in the sky above earth's equator. At these times the center of the sun spends approximately equal amounts of time above and below the horizon, making night and day of equal lengths. These solar events, combined with the summer and winter solstices, mark our seasons. For those of us in the northern hemisphere the movement of the sun southward past the equator signals the beginning of fall. After today, the sun will continue its trajectory and our days will grow shorter until we reach December 21, the winter solstice.

The fall equinox, like all the other celestial markers, has many interesting symbolic interpretations. I like the idea of balance between dark and light which can be understood both literally and psychologically. All of us have endured dark times as well as times when a lighter mood prevailed. We know what it is to search for a balance between despair and hope, especially in times of chaos and uncertainty. Throughout our lives we struggle to find balance between those attitudes or behaviors that are beneficial to our growth and those that are detrimental. We often swing between negative feelings and more positive ones, always hoping to find equilibrium. We can get caught up in habitual patterns that do not serve us well but that are hard to change even though we know that we need to find a way to moderate them.

At my stage of life I am still searching for a wholesome balance in my life. Do I spend too much time alone or too little? Do I watch too many political programs on TV? Would I be better off watching movies? Or just sitting in my garden? Or reading? Do I have the right amount of social activities? Do I exercise enough? Am I too serious? Do I find time for fun? For those in a younger generation, such as working Moms and Dads, there is the constant effort to find a balance between responsibilities to career and to family and self. Later, it is finding the proper balance between work and retirement. The poet May Sarton uses the word *poise* to describe the sense of having our lives in balance. For most of us there is constant vacillation, something like walking on a balance beam, veering somewhat unsteadily from one side and the other, being careful not to lean too far in either direction.

Another characteristic of fall is that it is harvest time. Traditionally to harvest means to reap, gather, and store grain and other crops from the fields. Harvest is celebrated throughout the world in a variety of ways. Here in the United States we have Thanksgiving; Jews have Succoth, which this year falls on September 23. In Greek mythology it marked a change in season, the time Persephone returned to the underworld for three months to be with her husband Hades.

Aspects of our lives can be harvested as well. What ideas

were planted in the past year that have now grown into fruition? What goals have been reached? What accomplishments acknowledged? What projects completed? What additions have we made to our lives? What insights have we garnered? It is worthwhile to take time to ponder these things, to take stock, to take measure of our inner and outer productivity. If the crops of our lives have not been rewarding or effective, it might be a good time to reflect on the reasons. Perhaps we can make some changes. If we have reason to be proud of our achievements, then it is time for celebration.

Fall also represents a time of approaching dormancy, a period when growth and development temporarily stops. The tender plants of summer cannot withstand the cold and frost that come with the decline in hours of sunlight and the decrease in temperature. Perennials die back, becoming dormant until the spring warmth returns. Bulbs store nutrients, ready to bloom once again in the spring. Some animals hibernate, reserving their energy for warmer weather when more food is available. They accomplish this by lowering their metabolic rate and their body temperature.

The autumnal equinox can also remind us that fall and the coming of winter represent a transition time for our inner and outer lives, a time to lessen our usual frenetic mental and physical activity, to settle down, to talk less and listen more, to go inward, to conserve our energy for later times. There is much to be gained by slowing down for a little while.

For me, of course, now ninety years old, autumn has special poignance. Though by age I should think of myself as being in the last season of my life, I feel more as if I am still in late fall, nearing winter. I am reminded of something I wrote twenty-five years ago, called "Flowers that Bloom in the Fall." I read it at a ritual attended by women in their middle to late years. In it I likened the seasons to the life spans of women. I pointed out that the spring is the time of the young woman, whose beauty unfolds like the petals of a rose, whose innocence and purity is akin to the lily, whose delicacy and sweetness are like cherry blossoms, and whose fire and vigor are like the splendor of a bed of red tulips.

I explained that summer brings an abundance of flowers: petunias and zinnias and cosmos and begonias and sunflowers. Several women in in that group were in the summer of their lives—writing plays and books and getting degrees and advancing in their careers. They also were the blooms resulting from mothering children and grandchildren and represented the beauty of living life fully and well.

But what about fall? I used the occasion to remind them that it is important for all of us to keep in mind that as we reach the fall of our lives we need not stop blooming. I had brought a bouquet of yellow chrysanthemums, so I pointed out that each one of us has gifts as full and as spectacular as those gorgeous golden chrysanthemums. Some of us, I said, may find that our most beautiful blossoms are produced at this late stage of our lives. We may finally burst into bloom with enormous gusto, with brilliance even, or we may unfold more quietly. However it happens, I said, I wish to remind you: Do not despair if you feel fall approaching. Flowers bloom in the fall.

JULY 2018

Love

What is love? Why do we fall in love with one person, but not another? What ignites that fire of desire? How do we understand the love, pride and adoration we feel for our children and grandchildren—and in my case, great-grandchildren? What attracts us to our friends? What does it mean to fall in love with ourselves? What causes our hearts to swoon at the beauties of nature? How can we learn to embrace every living, or even non-living, thing with love?

Carl Jung spoke of "the incalculable paradoxes of love." In his memoir, *Memories, Dreams, Reflections,* he confessed that "in my own life I have again and again been faced with the mystery of love, and have never been able to explain what it is." If Jung could not figure it out, it is perhaps foolhardy for me to undertake such a complicated, impossible-to-define topic. But I am intrigued by the challenge.

I know that I experience love, but I love people in different ways and for different reasons. I know love that involves sexual passion, and love that is nonsexual; sometimes it is a complex mixture of the two. I know love for both men and women, for those related to me and those who are friends. Occasionally I am struck with a strange attraction—love?—to someone I barely know. I do not have a pet, but I know that intense feelings of love exist between dogs, cats, horses, and other animals and their owners.

I have an inexpressible, profound love for my garden. On a few transitory occasions I have felt an immediate, ineffable love that encompasses all beings. All these feelings are real and powerful, but how to describe the differences? We English-speakers are limited to that one overloaded, overused word *love* for this divergent, dynamic aspect of our emotional lives.

The ancient Greeks, on the other hand, had seven categories of love. First was *Eros*, love of the body, including sexual desire, described as a kind of madness, such as falling madly in love. Second was *Philia*, love of the mind, what we think of as platonic love, such as that between friends. Third was *Storge*, the love that exists between parents and children, a familial love. Fourth was *Agape*, altruism, love of nature, or universal love, as for God. Fifth was *Ludus*, a playful love, suggesting teasing, flirting, seducing. Sixth was *Pragma*, what might be thought of as a pragmatic arrangement when sexual love yields to more practical considerations, such as shared goals. Arranged marriages would be in this category. And finally, *Philautia*, self-love, which is beneficial, but can lead to hubris.

Though I can relate to most of these categories (though not *Ludus* and *Pragma*), I am not sure my feelings of love can easily fit into these defined groups. They overlap and blend. For example, I think of *Eros* as a life force that can be expressed not only sexually but in our enthusiasms. It is a source of power that can overwhelm us. My initial attraction to my husband was something I have called "intellectual eroticism." I was enthralled by his intellect, seduced by his knowledge of scientific and philosophical ideas, characteristics I had never encountered before. I still find a thoughtful approach to life immensely appealing, erotic in this sense. I look for it in my relationships; intellectualism stimulates my mind and arouses my curiosity. Though it is "love of the mind," it seems of a different quality than the Greek *Philia*, platonic love. Platonic love, at least to me, implies an emotional neutrality, lacking the warmth and intensity that I experience.

The love that exists among family members the Greeks called *Storge*, a natural or instinctual affection. We first learn about love and its many permutations from our primary family, but family interactions are notoriously complicated. As has been said, somewhat facetiously, "the function of families is to be dysfunctional." The love that exists between parents and children, between siblings, or between grandparents and grandchildren varies; each has its inherent constraints. As parents we carry the burden of responsibility for our children. We love them, but we also want them to reflect well on us. Siblings may be competitive with each other, reflecting real or imagined favoritism. In my experience, the purest form of family love is that which flows between grandparent and grandchild. As grandparents we are relieved of the awesome accountability that rests on parents and can therefore offer unqualified love and acceptance of each grandchild's life path.

The Greeks also recognized self-love or *Philautia*. Psychologically it is important that we have a healthy regard for our worthiness. Like any form of love, however, it has its dark side, which is narcissism. Narcissism involves an exaggerated view of one's abilities and an incessant desire for admiration. It results in extreme selfishness, having little or no empathy or understanding of the needs of others. (We have a supreme example in Trump, our current president.)

One of the most fascinating kinds of love is *Agape*, a love that is unconditional and universal. It represents the ultimate goal, that of loving without any expectation of return and without any judgment; it persists independent of any circumstance. It is transcendent, and is frequently described by mystics as a feeling of oneness, being lovingly connected to everything in the universe. Persons who have had near-death experiences relate being welcomed into another realm with total acceptance and love. Many who have taken psychedelics report an overwhelming feeling that love is the most powerful force on the planet.

Buddhists have a *metta* prayer or meditation that focuses on lovingkindness, a practice that helps develop compassion and an unconditional love that extends to all beings. One version begins by wishing love, good health, safety, well-being, and happiness on ourselves, for unless we accept and love ourselves it is difficult to extend it to others. Next we include those closest to us, then strangers; after that, those with whom we have difficulties; and finally we extend this love to the world at large. This is the ideal, selfless love, which each of us, theoretically, has the potential to realize.

In writing this brief essay on such a huge topic, I have come across some memorable passages regarding the nature of love. One is a famous quote by the French philosopher, Jesuit priest, and paleontologist Pierre Teilhard de Chardin.

> *The day will come when, after harnessing the ether, the winds, the tides, gravitation, we shall harness for God the energies of love. And, on that day, for the second time in the history of the world, man will have discovered fire.*

Kahlil Gibran, in his book The Prophet, uses striking images to remind us that in our most intimate, loving relationships we must allow room for change, growth, individuality, and solitude.

> *Sing and dance together and be joyous, but let each one of you be alone,*
> *Even as the strings of a lute are alone though they quiver with the same music.*
> *Give your hearts, but not into each other's keeping.*
> *For only the hand of Life can contain your hearts.*

> *And stand together... yet not too near together:*
> *For the pillars of the temple stand apart,*
> *And the oak tree and the cypress grow not in each other's shadow.*

One of the most beautiful commentaries on love is found in I Corinthians, 1-8:

> *If I speak in the tongues of mortals and of angels, but do not have love, I am a noisy gong or a clanging cymbal.*
> *And if I have prophetic powers and understand all mysteries and all knowledge, and if I have all faith, so as to remove mountains, but do not have love, I am nothing.*
> *If I give away all my possessions, and if I hand over my body so that I may boast, but do not have love, I gain nothing.*

> *Love is patient; love is kind; love is not envious or boastful or arrogant or rude. It does not insist on its own way; it is not irritable or resentful; it does not rejoice in wrongdoing, but rejoices in the truth.*
>
> *It bears all things, believes all things, hopes all things, endures all things.*
>
> *Love never ends.*

Jung was right. Love is mysterious, full of "incalculable paradoxes." I am awed by it, utterly incapable of describing the elusive sensations it invokes in me. Though I am fortunate to be loved by many, my desire for love seems endless. Perhaps that is due to my early deprivation of motherlove, which can never be fully compensated. During our long marriage I frequently urged my late husband to occasionally say "I love you," but he could never utter those words spontaneously, causing me great sadness. Maybe this yearning for more love is a universal human condition, experienced by all of us. I also wish that I could express my love for others in a more generous, sincere, and unguarded manner, saying "I love you" more frequently without the words becoming stale and meaningless. In these final years of my life, I long to reach deeper into the mystery of love, to love and be loved without restraint.

OCTOBER 2018

Soup

A week or so ago, a sudden change in weather from 90 degrees to cold and rainy days aroused in me a desire to make soup. I find preparing this particular dish to be profoundly grounding and fulfilling. Perhaps it is because I relate to Hestia, the Greek goddess of the hearth and home, that I find such immense pleasure in bringing together the varied ingredients that produce a hearty, soul-satisfying soup. It is not only nourishing fare for the body, but also beneficial for the spirit. Just as the slow-burning fire on Hestia's hearth provided a sense of stability and continuity for the ancient family domicile, making soup in my modern kitchen provides me with an anchor of sorts, offering a calmer, more contemplative frame of mind.

In this era of fast food, soup is decidedly a "slow" food. It takes time to make a good soup. It is a deliberative process, often demanding more than one stage of preparation. First is gathering the ingredients for making a stock, the foundation of a good soup. Whether chicken, beef, or vegetarian, the stock must have a variety of components, including vegetables and herbs, to assure a rich, viscous texture and flavor. It must be cooked slowly, simmered at the subtle temperature just below boiling. I often prepare this a day or two before I make whatever soup is planned, or freeze it for later use. My house recently smelled of delicious chicken stock.

Then comes assembling the elements for the soup itself, whether it is vegetable, bean, or one of my family's preferred vegetarian ones, spinach. Last week I made bean soup, with onions, carrots, celery, and red peppers, flavored with ham hocks. A few days later I made broccoli and potato soup, seasoned with dill and buttermilk. Then I made spinach soup, enhanced by a bit of garlic and a generous amount of nutmeg. All are favorites, and will go into the freezer for our Thanksgiving gathering.

I see a parallel between the slow cooking required in making soup and the exquisitely measured process, often painfully lengthy and laborious, of merging our disparate, sometimes conflicting, traits into a fully formed human. Just as stock slowly melds together a variety of flavors, so the observations, experiences, insights, and knowledge that we acquire along the years of our lives coalesce to make us who we are. It is in gradually "cooking" our raw, undeveloped characteristics and attitudes that we are transformed into more seasoned, coherent, and compassionate selves.

Another reason I find such pleasure in preparing soup is that it reminds me of the many past Thanksgivings when we as a family have come together, sharing traditional Thanksgiving fare, including soup that I have prepared. In addition to being physically nourishing and flavorful, and being analogous to our personal development, I think of soup as a metaphor for the blending of our family members. We are of different ages and backgrounds, each with his or her distinctive temperament and eccentricities, yet we mingle and meld into a compatible, comforting, stimulating assemblage. Like fine ingredients and tasty herbs that combine to make a delicious soup, we merge into a mellow mélange of fun, compassion, hope, and love. It is an astonishing occurrence and a great blessing, making Thanksgiving my favorite holiday.

APRIL 2019

Homes

Norm and I shared many homes during our marriage of almost sixty years. I realize that many of you, especially my grandchildren, have scant knowledge of most of these places. So, for what it may be worth, I have been delving into my memory, attempting to distill some small essence of what our lives were like at each of those homes.

When Norm and I married in September, 1948, at the beginning of our senior year at Washington University, Norm's brother Al and his wife Lennie most generously offered us a room in their house on DeGiverville in St. Louis. In exchange, we prepared dinners and babysat their two young daughters. We painted our tiny room blue. I still remember the design of the gray bedspread we had on the bed, which pretty much filled the room. The house was not far from the university, so we either walked or took the streetcar to school. Sharing a home with a family of four had its challenges, but we were grateful for a chance to be together.

After we graduated and Norm was accepted into a graduate program at the University of Iowa, we put an ad in the Iowa City paper for an apartment. We received one response—from the director of the campus YMCA and his wife—for a basement apartment at their home. We were relieved to have found a place to live, but when we arrived in late August, the floor of the basement apartment was covered in water, with huge chlorine bags hanging from the ceiling in an attempt to absorb the moisture. Not a very welcome sight for our very first apartment! There was no refrigerator, just an icebox, and a two-burner hotplate for cooking. We had very little money, at first living on Norm's GI bill payment of $105 per month, subsisting largely on pancakes made from packages of mix.

The family with two little boys lived on the first floor. We lived in the basement. Two Black students lived on the second floor because they were not allowed rooms in university dorms. We grew to be friends. When we invited one of them to come to St. Louis for Thanksgiving, we had to take along our own food for the journey because no restaurant along the way that would serve Blacks. Due to our different religious backgrounds, Norm and I were described by our landlord as the "mixed couple." I eventually got a job in the Dean's office, and later entered the Speech and Audiology Department. It was a time of struggle, study, and adjustment to a new way of life.

After a year in the basement apartment we moved into a trailer park owned by the university, open to married graduate students. It was conveniently close to campus, a great advantage, since our previous abode was six long blocks from the nearest bus, a freezing walk in Iowa winters. The accommodations were not, however, much of an improvement in terms of comfort. There was no running water in our very small trailer, so we took our dishes to a central washhouse to wash. When we needed to use the toilet or take a shower we had to walk to the communal bathhouse along the boards serving as sidewalks. Believe me, trips to the bathhouse, snow piled high on each side of the path, were unforgettable! But we had friends, another couple, who also lived in the trailer park. We decided on a cooperative arrangement; we took turns preparing dinner so that the other three could spend that time studying. As I remember, Norm knew how to cook only one dish, so we always knew what would be on the menu on his nights as chef. All meals were cooked on a two-burner hotplate. But it was really nice to share those times with friends.

After getting our master's degrees in February, 1952, Norm was offered a job at Electro-Voice, a company that manufactured commercial and hi-fi sound equipment, at the amazing annual salary of $3500. (We thought we were rich!) We moved into a new apartment building in Niles, Michigan, that had a real kitchen, real bathroom, and automatic heating! Such luxury! Both of us fell ill with colds immediately. We had no furniture, nor money to buy any. Our only substantial belongings were a typewriter and a sewing machine. The orange crates we had used to pack our few belongings became our table and chairs. We slept on the floor until Norm's boss, learning of our situation, kindly advanced us enough money to buy a bed and an unfinished chest of drawers. Eventually we were able to add a table, a couch and a couple of chairs. I made curtains from muslin, trimmed with a bit of colorful fabric. I was beginning to become a homemaker and Norm was beginning his career as an engineer.

I soon found a job in Elkhart, Indiana, at a preschool for handicapped children. It was a bit of a commute and involved traveling to a different time zone every day. Before long, with the addition of my salary, we had accumulated enough money to consider beginning a family. Once I became pregnant, we found a small three-bedroom, ranch-style home with a nice yard in Niles and moved in a couple of months before Laura was born, September, 1953. We bought a crib and I painted some small animal figurines to hang over it. I can still picture us standing there, looking expectantly, and perhaps a bit nervously, into the empty crib, waiting eagerly for its occupant. We were thrilled to become parents.

We stayed in that little house through Jenny's birth in 1955. She was born in nearby South Bend, Indiana, and I was the first mother to try a new procedure in that hospital, something called "rooming-in" which meant having the baby with you in the room. Previously all infants were kept in the nursery and brought in only at feeding times. I was thrilled to have my baby girl in a bassinet next to me. We were now a family of four. During our time in Niles, we became close friends with Erwin and Marge Gaede who lived in South Bend. Erv was the very liberal minister of the Unitarian church there. We often stayed after services to have lunch with them, for the house was used both as a sanctuary and as housing for the Gaede family. Though Erv and Marge have died, I have remained close to their daughter Susan and her daughter Maggie—three generations of friendship.

After a few years at Electro-Voice, Norm felt a need to move on. He was offered a job in Cedar Rapids, Iowa, where he felt his opportunities might be improved. In a sense that was true, for the Turner family, which owned an electronic business, also owned funeral homes, and Norm was asked, in addition to his knowledge of speakers and microphones, to occasionally explore some of the issues regarding the dynamics of embalming. We rented a coal-fired house on the grounds of the Turner factory, which was quite convenient; Norm could literally walk a few yards home for lunch. But it also meant dealing with the incredibly filthy air quality of a furnace constantly spewing coal dust into our home. Jenny, who was crawling at the time, had to be bathed and clothing changed frequently because of the grimy air which, come to think of it, all of us were breathing.

Our move to Cedar Rapids was short lived as we learned that Norm's father had been diagnosed with terminal lung cancer. We decided to move to St. Louis both to support Norm's family but also to provide our children with family connections which were non-existent between me and my family. We made the move even though Norm had no job in St. Louis.

We found a small apartment on Page Avenue. (It was here that we had our very first TV.) This was in the early 1950s, during the McCarthy era. Employees at any business having government contracts were required to sign a loyalty oath, something Norm refused to do. It was a discouraging time, as non-governmental jobs for a sound engineer seemed impossible to find. We were slowly using up all our savings when, driven by desperation, Norm applied for an ill-suited job as a lighting salesman. It turned out to be fortuitous, as the owner of the small business wanted to expand into sound products. To make a long story short, over time, this became Norm's business, Soundolier. As it became established, and by the time Laura was ready to go to kindergarten, we moved into a home on Partridge Avenue in University City.

The girls grew up there and graduated from University City high school. I worked at St. Joseph's Institute for the Deaf, and frequently brought children who were living in the dorm home for the weekend. Another important event took place during our years there. The first Black family to move into University City moved into a house across the street from us. George was an executive with Pepsi-Cola and Que was a school dietitian. When they moved in I took over a batch of cookies which was the start of a good friendship. Que and I visited back and forth between our homes almost every day. It was the early 1960s, a time when residential and school segregation were undergoing dramatic changes. It is depressing to realize that all these many years later, many of those patterns of discrimination still persist.

I had always wanted to live in the country, so as our daughters approached their senior year in high school, I started looking for a lot not too far from the city. I saw an ad for one that was described as likely to appeal to those who "marched to the beat of a different drum." That caught my eye immediately and we drove out to look at it. At the time, the lot of five wooded, hilly acres in a community of widely spaced homes called Lakewood Hills, was inaccessible by car. But it was just what I wanted. We bought it and began going out on weekends to picnic on the property. Soon afterwards I began working with an architect to design my dream house. I loved the process of helping make esthetic and practical decisions. We found a local builder to do the construction and just before the girls went off to college we moved in. I loved that house, located "of the hill," up a curving driveway, with its cedar exterior and dramatic sculptural shape, nestled among the trees. It was an extraordinary home, both inside and out. I reveled in it.

Though Norm had agreed to all our decisions, I don't think he ever felt comfortable living in the country, nor did the house satisfy him esthetically as it did me. He was raised in the city, so country sounds, such as noisy whippoorwills at night and the challenges of navigating the narrow, hilly roads in bad weather, made him extremely anxious. Eventually we rented a small apartment in town so that we could have a place to stay when he felt especially uneasy or concerned by the threat of inclement weather. We were staying there so much that we moved to a larger place so our children would have room when they visited. At that time Norm was entering a period of deep depression, something that lasted a few years after he sold his company. Those were very trying, painful times.

Norm sold the company in 1983 which gave us enough money to buy a large condo, my current home, where I have lived for more than 35 years. In selling the company, he had agreed to travel to New Jersey every other week to supervise blending his company with that of another in Parsippany. We bought a small garden apartment in West Orange, an easy commute to his work but in the opposite direction of New York City. Those were exciting years as I became familiar with the museums, theater, galleries, and restaurants in the city. In time, Norm found his new role extremely draining, so when his agreement ended we stayed at the apartment just for special visits with family or friends. Eventually we realized we were barely using it, so we sold it and bought an apartment in Chicago, since most of our family were living in the Midwest at that time.

As our second home, which Norm humorously referred to as our "winter getaway" since more sensible people preferred Florida, we purchased a two-bedroom condo on the 55th floor of the John Hancock Building. It was a beautiful space with a stunning view along the north shore of Lake Michigan. Not long after we bought that place I decided to enter analysis with a Jungian analyst near the city, so I drove to Chicago at least once a month, often alone, for many years. I loved being there, even though the analytic process brought up many troubling issues in both my relationship with my mother and in my marriage. Examining one's conflicts can be painful, and I shed buckets of tears during those five-hour drives back and forth from St. Louis. But I did grow in my sense of self, and due to the guidance I received, I was able to enroll in a graduate program at Pacifica Graduate Institute at age 69. That was a major development in the later years of my life.

After the sale of Soundolier, we also acquired a lakeside property near Webb Lake, Wisconsin. I had a rather ridiculous fantasy that this place, with its accommodations for multiple families, would become a kind of family compound, with all of us throughout the years gathering for holidays and special occasions. And we did come together there for quite a few years at Thanksgiving, when we established the tradition of having a yearly Thanksgiving ritual. We also had coming-of-age ceremonies there for our granddaughters Jessica and Rachel. During our times there the grandchildren did projects, played dress-up, put on plays, and participated in their own sibling dramas. But as they grew older, the youngsters and their families developed their own priorities regarding where to spend their free time. The Webb Lake property was not working out as I had envisioned, so we handed over the deed to daughter Jenny, since it was most convenient to her family in Minneapolis. It remains a beautiful spacious cabin on the shores of a lovely lake, now largely serving the needs of Jenny, her family, and their friends.

As Norm's health declined, and my analyst retired, we were no longer making those trips to Chicago. With some reluctance, I sold our unit there. The same thing with the Lakewood Hills house, which we kept even after moving into my present home. I would often go out there alone, but even those trips became infrequent, so I made the decision to sell that house.

When I look back over the plethora of dwellings we have inhabited, I am rather astonished. Some, of course, were due to career moves to different cities, and several of the later ones were second homes, never our primary dwelling. Each purchase had a rationale, and each one brings back a flood of memories, both positive and negative. Our time in each had its own unique combination of struggles, accomplishments, trials, sorrows, and delights. I have learned that life is a series of ups and downs, with hopefully, a steady spiraling upward as we learn to cope with life's inevitable challenges.

Now, thankfully, I am responsible for only one living space, one that I have come to love ever more deeply over the years. It is convenient to the airport and other places of interest, has a small garden which nourishes my soul, and is large enough to accommodate guests and family gatherings. It serves my needs perfectly, and it is my hope to remain here as long as possible. Since I am now ninety years old, I am quite aware that there may soon come a time when I must move where I can be provided with additional care. But for now I am happy to be here—still on this earth and in this warm and comforting home.

THANKSGIVING 2018
WILD, WARM, AND WONDERFUL

There were eighteen of us this year for our Thanksgiving celebration. It is my favorite holiday, a time to focus on family, without the extra layer of expectation and obligation brought on by the exchange of gifts. Beginning in 1992, now more than twenty-five years ago, we have celebrated the occasion by joining in a ritual focused on some theme related to the concept of giving. We are together for the entire weekend, which allows us time for additional activities and projects.

Initially there was some trepidation about the idea of having a family ritual. Perhaps it was too hokey, or too new-agey, or too religious. Disregarding those doubts, I sent out a letter a month or so in advance and outlined my thoughts on what would be a good way for us to avoid the often superficial conversation that can dominate many family gatherings. I suggested that we set up a family altar, where each person would place something that represented an important event of the past year. We would talk about those items, thus sharing with each other something significant from our lives.

I also suggested that each of us complete the following sentences:

I am thankful for _____.
I am thankful that I am _____.

I am thankful that I have _____.
I am thankful that I can_____.

In addition I asked that each of us name one or more persons at the table and thank them for some special kindness or express gratitude for something learned from them.

I opened the ritual, which took place around the table between dinner and dessert, with honoring of the elements. I provided an example of each— a rock for earth, a feather for air, a candle for fire, and a shell for water—for each family member. I wished to instill in them an appreciation for the symbols used in many spiritual traditions. Though we are not a conventionally religious family, I wanted us to value the spiritual aspects of our lives.

Though it was a new experience for us, my sense is that all of us found it of great value. I became aware that my grandchildren have an instant comfort with ceremony. They participated with great interest, even enthusiasm, for children have a natural affinity for drama and play. They indulged their imagination and creativity. One of them, Jessie, who was nine at the time, read a poem she had written honoring the elements.

So began our tradition, all those many years ago, which continues to this day. We have focused on many different themes, among which were Harvest, at which we talked about what we had harvested in our lives and what we might like to harvest in the future. Another was Gratitude and Generosity, prompting a discussion about how these terms are related, how we might develop greater generosity and then expressed gratitude for each person seated at the table.

Another time, at the suggestion of my husband who was then immersed in a study of physics, we addressed the concept of Interconnectedness and what it means to feel connected to one another. We also talked about how awful it feels to be disconnected. As a special project we made lifelines. I gave a yard-long cord to each person, and provided miniature objects and clay which could be shaped into symbolic representations of important life events. These objects were then attached to the cord. As each of us shared our lifeline, we then tied them all together, demonstrating our connectedness as a family.

On yet another Thanksgiving, we talked about the importance of Family—what it means to us, how our family is unusual, and what we value most. Jenny made a large family tree which we mounted on the wall so we could see the generations of our family history. In a similar vein a few years ago we talked about Family Ties. For this one we distributed short lengths of ribbons, a different color to each person. Then each of us tied one of our ribbons to everyone else's color, and as we did so, spoke of our relationship with that person. All the joined ribbons created a beautiful collection symbolic of our close ties as a family. I placed those in a small basket which has remained on my coffee table since that time.

When great-grandchildren arrived, it seemed imperative to find themes that they could understand. I wanted them to experience at an early age the importance of participating in this family tradition. At some of our recent Thanksgivings we have talked about Sharing, Helping, and Kindness, topics persons of all ages can comprehend and appreciate. We also have done projects such as preparing gift bags for children in homeless shelters, and providing goods for recently arrived immigrants. These projects were meant to demonstrate our understanding of the discussion by doing something concrete to bring more meaning to our ritual.

This year another innovation has taken place—a most welcome one. Granddaughters Rebecca and Carolyn offered to conduct our traditional Thanksgiving ritual. It began by five-year-old Ella and her three-year-old brother Sawyer singing "The More We Get Together…The Happier We'll Be." (I think we should adopt this as our annual theme song.) We then were given lengths of yarn which we tied together to form a continuous circle, defining the safe space for our ritual.

The topic Carolyn and Rebecca chose was not only timely, but important for us to consider: Activism. In this time of political turmoil, when the divisions in our country are becoming more and more worrying, it seemed essential that we learn how best to take on those troublesome issues and causes that are necessary for the preservation of our democracy. They posed the following questions for us to think about:

- Does activism have to be visible? How is today's activism the same or different from the street activism of previous generations?
- How do you combat apathy and tuning out?
- People often say armchair activism is bad; is it? Are there ways to make it more involved?

- What does introverted activism look like?
- Sustaining activism is hard. What are strategies for how to maintain passion?
- Does it help to know you are part of a movement?
- How has activism changed with age in our own lives?
- If you are happy with your level of activism, how have you stayed motivated? If you are not, what are the challenges or things keeping you from what you wish you did?
- We are in a time of political upheaval. What does activism look like (or does it matter) in more peaceful times?
- What causes are you actively involved with? How have you chosen those?
- What does activism look like in other countries?

We had a long, lively, interesting discussion based on these questions. This topic obviously was meaningful to our family members. Though we have always been interested in politics, this was an opportunity for us to examine ways in which we might more effectively express our liberal views. The great-grandchildren talked about taking part in protest marches. We also put together hygiene kits—soap, shampoo, toothbrushes and toothpaste, combs, deodorant—for those in homeless shelters.

It was especially meaningful to me that my grandchildren chose to carry on our family tradition of giving serious consideration to significant matters. It was a confirmation of what I had always hoped for in our family gatherings: that in an atmosphere of safety and comfort, we would get beyond superficialities and engage in thoughtful conversation about ideas of both personal and general consequence.

One final note on our 2018 Thanksgiving: Wild because the great-grandchildren are energetic, creative, and enthusiastic in their play, making for a boisterous, somewhat chaotic atmosphere. Warm because there is a palpable feeling of love and acceptance among all family members, with frequent expressions of affection. Wonderful because at age ninety I am lucky enough to have lived to experience the joy of celebrating yet another Thanksgiving with those I love most—my family.

CONNECTING

JANUARY 2019

Writing

In an earlier reflection, *An Alternative Self*, I shared a fantasy about seeing my former professor Chris Downing's life as a replacement for my own. In the introduction to her most recent book I was touched by how similar her goals were to what I have aimed for in my own reflections. She wrote that her essays were all about her, that they helped her understand herself, helped her become herself. I feel the same way about my writings. Among the essays in her book was one titled "Alphabet Magic." It impressed me because, again, she touched on a topic that resonates with me and which prompts me to examine some of my own feelings, in this case about writing.

In her essay Downing gives a comprehensive, scholarly history of the development of the alphabet. The earliest symbols were pictograms, invented in Mesopotamia around 3200 BCE. It is not known just when consonant alphabets (those which represent sound as emerging from the body of the speaker) were first developed, but by the 11th century the Phoenicians had developed a cursive alphabet of 22 characters that the Hebrews and other Canaanite peoples adopted. The inclusion of symbols for vowels came later.

Downing describes how in the Talmudic period (first and second centuries CE) the Hebrew letters, especially those of the divine name YHVH, were considered as having magical power. The kabbalists, those who follow a mystical religious interpretation of Judaism, view these four letters as an image of God and assert that the six permutations of the four letters formed the first level of created order and that the other letters completed the formation of the material universe. While a bit much to comprehend, the point is, as Downing writes, "The letters are the building blocks, which were only subsequently combined to form the words and then sentences of the Torah. Thus the Torah is the instrument through which the world came into being." According to this view, writing is the foundation of our world.

In our era of mass communication it is almost impossible to imagine a time when texts did not exist. Oral traditions, story-telling, therapeutic and other kinds of personal conversations are vitally important, but require face-to-face (or virtual) encounters. In contrast, writing allows our thoughts and observations to be shared with those far away and can be perused repeatedly if necessary or desired. Our spoken words are largely ephemeral (less so now with recording devices), but words that are written have the possibility of a more lasting impact, of approaching permanence. The texts of ancient philosophers, prophets, and poets continue to provide us with guidance and insights regarding ethics, metaphysics, logic, ontology, theology, politics, and other fields of study. It was, for example, centuries ago that Plato informed us of Socrates' famous words uttered at the trial at which he was sentenced to death, "The unexamined life is not worth living." I, for one, continue to examine my life as best I can.

I am intrigued and challenged by the process of writing, fascinated by our ability to use words to question and explore.

As I have said before, sharing my thoughts with others through these written reflections provides me an opportunity to search for what is most meaningful to me as I live out my later years. As Downing puts it, "How can we *not* want to use those magic symbols to say, to write, our own souls into being!" She correctly points out that writing "is discovery, is creation,...is erotic—it is a way of reaching out to the souls of others, others whom we may never meet but whom we are addressing nonetheless." As I write my reflections, I am learning something new about myself, something formerly overlooked or dismissed or unidentified. As I unearth and reveal those formerly veiled or concealed characteristics, I am creating a new vision of myself. Like Downing, I find that writing is erotic, sensuous, for I definitely feel a surge of energy and excitement—*eros*—when I am engaged in assembling these little essays.

I am also expressing my desire for deeper connection—"reaching out to the souls of others." It is a way of both enriching and confirming my relationship with those who read my words. Most often I am addressing the people closest to me, family members or dear friends, though I am certainly not averse to having strangers as my readers. As I write, I am hoping that my observations might resonate with, reinforce, or relate to some of the thoughts or experiences of others. There undoubtedly will be disagreements with my perspectives, but that only adds to my hopeful expectation that those differences will motivate those who disagree to seriously examine some of their own assumptions. What I have to say might both add to their understanding of who I am and also provide greater insight into their own thinking.

As with many who risk sharing their thoughts and baring their souls on the written page, I experience an undeniable anxiety that what I write may be overly self-indulgent, or shallow, or repetitious. I know I am likely to revisit certain themes, that I am not always capable of going deep enough. I must frequently remind myself to be as honest as I can be without seeming too confessional, and I often regret that I am not as astute as I would wish. But, I tell myself, I am trying! I am probing, delving, attempting to plunge into the depths of my consciousness, hoping to live these final years of my life with as much authenticity and integrity as I can. Perhaps sharing my effort will inspire others to do the same.

All of this depends on "alphabet magic," or what I think of as the magic of words. It is the endless variety of combination of letters that makes possible the formation of words, sentences, paragraphs, essays such as the one I am now writing. While we must be alert that words can be used to defame and denigrate, it is important that we recognize how carefully worded phrases can make fresh connections and can facilitate our understanding of complex and controversial issues. The expressions we choose can help create new realities, both for ourselves and for others. The poet Mary Oliver, who died recently, is quoted as saying in an interview regarding the abusive household in which she grew up, "I made a world out of words. And it was my salvation." She reminds us that we can salvage hope from despair through our use of words, a magic much needed in our world today.

SEPTEMBER 2019

Our Salon

One of my great pleasures is participating in a group that meets every other month or so and identifies itself as a Salon. I looked up the definition and this is what I found: "A *salon* is a gathering of people under the roof of an inspiring host, held partly to amuse one another and partly to refine the taste and increase the knowledge of the participants through conversation." I think that is a pretty accurate description of what goes on at our gatherings, since we do have "an inspiring host," though I am not entirely sure about our desire "to refine the taste." I feel our members already have quite exquisite tastes! But I know that we wish to explore ideas and increase our knowledge about philosophical concepts and current events through conversation. We most certainly do amuse each other—at least in the sense that we are entertained, made to think and to laugh.

It was Harriet's idea, and all of us welcomed it. She, along with her partner Anna, has remained our inspiring host for not only our discussions, but also for most of our dinners, though we do supplement her sumptuous main dish with offerings of our own. But it is the diverse but congenial group that makes the evenings so special. Though, as usual, I am the oldest (in my nineties) others are in their fifties, sixties, seventies, and eighties—a broad age range. Some are still working, others retired. Our backgrounds and professions are also varied: an artist, a professor of philosophy, a retired banker, a nutritionist, a professor of sexual health and education, a chef and restauranteur, a retired career counselor, a poet and playwright, a retired businessman, and a retired owner of a PR firm. We are Catholic, Jewish, Protestant, and none of the above. We are straight, gay, married, widowed, and divorced, sometimes several of these.

Our topics have ranged from a discussion of capitalism and democracy, truth (led by our philosopher), a sharing of reflections on a topic of our choosing, a consideration of immigration policies, a dialogue on sexual mores (guided by our sex specialist), a consideration of psychedelics, and others that I cannot recall. All have been lively and thought-provoking. At the beginning of each meeting we go around the circle doing a "check-in," which is a way of catching up on what is going on in each of our lives. As we have come to know each other better, our trust has deepened and this time of sharing has become more personal and meaningful. These exchanges are made possible due to an atmosphere of respect, appreciation, and affection. In that sense we are also an informal support group.

For those of us who are retired or no longer very active, it is especially valuable having the opportunity to listen to the perspectives of a group of well-informed friends, some of whom are still working, or are involved in interesting activities. The amount of knowledge and intellect represented is impressive, and the novel pursuits, often new ones following retirement, are inspiring. It is remarkable how these men and women continue to be engaged with life. They travel, care for grandchildren, write poems and plays and biographies, garden, teach, cater for large and small crowds, make art, make music, seriously meditate, and on and on. They serve as examples of how enriched our lives can be regardless of age.

So I feel compelled to address this to my fellow Salon members: I feel privileged to be a part of this amazing group. Each one of you has something to teach me. I know that some of you have endured great loss with courage and strength, or have met challenges within your families, or have dealt with personal health issues, or have struggled in your relationships, or in your work, or in more than one of these categories. But your enthusiasm is contagious, your commitment to the group is admirable, and your ability to offer support and encouragement is outstanding. I shall always be grateful for your insights and information. So, I thank all of you! It is my hope to remain with you as long as my mind and body permit.

AUGUST 2019

Unlikely Friends

Friends are usually people with whom we share common experiences, backgrounds, traits, ages, or interests. In most cases these relationships are built over a period of time as we slowly get to know each other. But occasionally chance encounters ignite a connection that results in unexpected and unlikely friendships. In those happenstances there is no need to explore the usual areas of commonality; somehow the attraction is instantaneous and real. A bond is immediately forged.

It is unclear what prompts these sudden attractions to individuals about whom we know very little. What mysterious quality transcends or abrogates the generally understood necessity for more deliberate considerations of friendship? The persons I have met and formed an instant attachment to frequently have backgrounds not at all like mine. We follow dissimilar pursuits and are of different generations. Perhaps by examining my relationship with a few of them I can get some insight into what it is that connects us.

Tim is the friend I have known longest. I met him when he came to help with a dinner party I was giving, perhaps in the mid 1980s. I was struck with his pleasant demeanor and the apparent ease and efficiency with which he carried out his duties that evening. When the guests left, we talked and a friendship blossomed. He quickly became a guest rather than a helper, though as a chef and caterer he often has been both, providing many wonderful meals for special occasions at my home.

Tim is Catholic, gay, and the approximate age of my daughters, but none of these differences has determined the parameters of our relationship. On the contrary, they have provided stimulating material for our many conversations. His spirituality transcends the doctrines of his church, and it is to his credit that he has found a way to maintain his personal integrity while adhering to the principles of love, morality, and generosity. To an outsider, it might appear that we have a mother-son relationship, but that has never been the case. I am sure I speak for both of us when I say that we see each other as peers, regardless of our age difference. We delight in sharing good meals and interesting discussions. I love him deeply and am blessed to have him in my life.

Another example is my friend Bidisha, whom I met in a most unlikely way. We were standing next to each other in a very long line waiting to go through security at the airport. She was heading to New York and I was heading to San Diego. We began to talk, and I was impressed with her enthusiasm, charm, and intelligence. I had an undeniable urge to get to know this young woman, so as we were about to go our separate ways, I handed her my card, and suggested that we stay in touch. While I was still in San Diego, I got an email from her, and we arranged to get together upon our return home. So began our friendship.

Bidisha was born in India, came to the U.S. for graduate school and is currently a professor of finance at St. Louis University. Her mother was born in 1950, and since I was married in 1948, technically she could be a granddaughter. Our backgrounds, cultures, ages, families, and fields of study are so different that it would seem we have little grounds for friendship. And yet, for many years we have kept in touch, sharing the events of our lives. I adore her.

And then there is Dara. She works for the landscape company that takes care of my garden. I do not know her age, but she is young—maybe still in her twenties. Sometimes her hair is purple, or sometimes she comes with a shaved head. No matter what, she is beautiful, energetic, always cheerful, a delight to see. When she can, she stays after the garden work is finished and has a cup of tea with me.

There is both a freshness and worldliness about Dara. From the little I know, she had a difficult childhood, but has worked hard to improve her situation. I admire her energy, her resourcefulness, and her resilience. She is in a serious relationship and has decided to go back to school to study nursing while continuing to work in landscaping part time. I admire her courage and her ambition. I love her and her youthful spirit.

Ellen is another unlikely friend, and yet another of my grandchildren's generation. When I met her she was a graduate student at the University of Missouri in St. Louis, studying clinical psychology, with a specialty in PTSD. Ellen is quiet and reserved, yet I was drawn to her, so would frequently invite her out to dinner with just the two of us. Several years ago, when she needed an attendant while undergoing minor surgery, and her mother was not available, I was pleased that she asked me to fill in. When she earned her PhD I hosted a party for her family and friends. When she moved out of town she found time to come for visits.

In a few months Ellen will marry Kate, an Episcopal priest, at a ceremony at St. James Cathedral in Chicago. I am lucky enough to be invited to the wedding! Ellen is a serious, yet delightful person, devoted to her partner, her work, and her family. I love her and am privileged to know her. In time I hope to get to know Kate. Perhaps she will become another unlikely friend.

My latest unlikely friend is a bartender, again, the age of my grandchildren. (I seem to be attracted to young people.) Kelly is fascinating, for he has a degree in political science and philosophy—not exactly the background one would expect of a bartender! He brings his intellect, conversational skill, and deep knowledge of wine and food into his exchanges with customers at the bar of an excellent restaurant near my home. This has become my favorite place to dine out—partly because the food is delicious, but also because when I enter, Kelly walks out from behind the bar and gives me a big hug. I do not know his wife or his extended family, but that does not diminish my love for this young man.

So, what are the qualities that attract me to this diverse group of people? One obvious factor is their willingness to engage with an old woman like me. They obviously have not fallen prey to the ageism and misogyny so prevalent in our society. They display an openness and readiness to explore new relationships. There is also an unmistakable warmth that permeates their being, melting the usual barriers between strangers. I find my horizons vastly extended and my heart expanded as I become better acquainted with these individuals whose lives are so different from mine. I listen to them and learn from them. I feel so lucky to have these unlikely friends, for each one has brought me joy and has enriched my life.

Relationships

JULY 2018

Perhaps it is understandable. On the cusp of ninety, I am beginning to reflect on my earlier reflections. A year ago I wrote a piece titled "Friends" which I am moved to examine from a different perspective. Most especially, I want to look more deeply into the intricacies of my relationship with my late husband. In what ways might it have affected how my friends viewed me? How did it impact how I perceived myself? I am also curious about what draws us to certain individuals, what role they play in our lives, and how we can best nurture those connections.

The Dalai Lama said, "Whether we like it or not, there is hardly a moment of our lives when we do not benefit from others' activities. So it is hardly surprising that most of our happiness arises in the context of our relationships with others." Though this is undoubtedly true, it is also true that relationships can bring us difficult, sometimes unresolvable, conflicts. Establishing, developing, and sustaining loving relationships demands time, patience, persistence, and compromise. Though not always easy, we keep trying, because the compensations are great.

Though I have now been a widow for more than ten years, I continue to think back on my marriage in order to get insights into what drew us together and what, at times, threatened our bond. (This account is how I experienced our marital life; Norm surely perceived it otherwise.) In spite of, or perhaps because of, our differences—he was Jewish, arrogant, intellectual, radical, and urban, whereas I was (former) Southern Baptist, modest, politically naïve, poorly educated, rural— we were powerfully attracted to each other. I was impressed with his intellect, smitten by his boldness, and captivated by his left-wing political views.

Our marriage took place despite strong objections from my family (I had to run away from home) and was a departure from religious and cultural standards of the time. Though we never had any religious conflicts, in 1948 it was rare for Jew and non-Jew marry. I was young, barely twenty, Norm twenty-two, both still undergraduates. We had few resources, lived off Norm's GI Bill benefits (available to veterans of World War II), $105 per month, and for the first year, relied on the kindness of Norm's brother who gave us a room in his home.

Given the disparities of our backgrounds, perhaps it was inevitable that we would face problems. There were numerous rough patches, many in our early years when we were struggling graduate students and I was trying to adjust to the changes in my life, which often brought on periods of depression. Through the years, though we had difficulties, we also had many good times. We settled in St. Louis, raised two delightful, intelligent daughters, did some traveling, shared homes in Michigan, Iowa, New Jersey, Chicago, Wisconsin. Our most serious issues arose after I entered analysis in my early sixties and began to assert myself as an equal and independent partner. Norm could not, or would not, discuss my desire for equality, but he began to suffer severe attacks of vertigo.

Obviously, I was turning his world upside down. During this period—after about forty-five years together—I seriously considered leaving the marriage. (I am certain he was ready to call it quits as well though he never said that to me.)

What I needed most was to be seen as someone other than Norm's wife, a partly self-imposed designation which nevertheless held me in its grip. (I had become a serious photographer, so it wasn't that I didn't have achievements.) Going back to school at age sixty-nine, earning a PhD, was a major step in finding my separate identity, but did not change Norm's narrow view of me as only mother and homemaker. Even after he began his decline into dementia, he persisted in referring to me as his "handy gadget." I chafed at that demeaning epithet, but by then I knew I was in for the long run. In spite of some perplexing, unresolved issues, we found a livable accommodation. I have always been extremely grateful that I stayed in the marriage. It was important for me to be there for him during those long, demanding, sad years of his illness. Confused as he was, I knew that he loved me and depended on me.

It was not until after his death that I was able to disentangle myself from Norm's powerful influence. It seems strange that it took so long for me to fully recognize my own abilities and strengths. They were there for all to see, but I could not see them myself. Only recently have I come to a significant insight regarding our complex relationship: My decision not to unequivocally demand equality was what allowed the marriage to survive. I understood at some level that Norm could not tolerate a true partnership, so I chose to keep intact a good, but not perfect, marriage. Our life together, however flawed, was complete: it prevailed, savoring joyful times and persisting through painful times. He died more than a decade ago, a few months short of what would have been our sixtieth wedding anniversary.

I am fortunate in having a few friends who knew us before Norm's illness and who supported me through our ups and downs. They remind me of the good times, recalling his intellect, his humor, and his generosity, characteristics blurred by memories of his later years of dementia. Though I struggled to disentangle myself from his overwhelming psychological and intellectual presence, I knew that these friends valued me as a separate human being; they saw beyond my function as "Norm's wife." Those friendships, so essential in helping me maintain my sense of self, continue to play an important role in my life. They give me a sense of continuity, connecting me to our shared past.

Perhaps because I felt under Norm's influence so strongly for so long, I am especially touched, and astonished, by the friendships I have formed in the decade since his death. I had not expected my range of friends to expand so significantly and in such diverse directions. My close relationships with men and women who never knew my husband have provided me with an unexpected infusion of energy and fulfillment. I know that I earned these friendships based solely on my own personhood, which makes them even more precious.

I am aware of several factors that draw me into a relationship. First, just as it was with Norm, is intellect. I like discussing ideas, current events, topics that are of common interest to me and my friends. I learn from their specialties, whether it be art or philosophy or social work or poetry or business.

I acquire new perspectives as I absorb information regarding their fields of study or career paths. I ask questions and am riveted by their enthusiasms. Their expertise helps correct some of my own ignorance or misunderstandings.

When I am with my friends we almost always talk about our families. I want to know what the children and grandchildren are doing, how parents and grandparents are faring, what problems they may be facing with siblings or in-laws. Sharing these personal stories is of primary importance, for it is in our most intimate relationships, such as that with our spouse or other family members, that we meet our greatest challenges. Listening to how my friends handle their difficulties often provides me with ideas about how to manage my own.

Another thing that draws me into a relationship is a willingness to discuss our innermost thoughts. I want to hear about longings, disappointments, anxieties, pleasures, how they feel about the mysteries of life and death. This kind of sharing involves a readiness to expose our vulnerabilities. If I feel safe enough to reveal my failures, and can confess my most shameful behavior without feeling judged, then I know I have a true friend. Out of that willingness to lay bare our weaknesses, knowing that we will still be accepted with love and understanding, grows the foundation of friendship, which is trust.

Along with the discussion of serious topics and the readiness to share fears and personal concerns, my friends and I spend a lot of our time together laughing. Our intimacy sparks some inner impishness or impertinence that enlivens our conversations. We do not tell jokes, but we find the absurdities of life to be amusing. We make fun of ourselves and laugh at each other's clever remarks. Laughter releases tensions and adds a sense of vitality; it is good for our health. I come away from these encounters with increased energy—a great gift.

There are, however, risks involved in any relationship. Sometimes we invest time and effort and love only to be mistreated, betrayed, or abandoned. In a marriage, illness, financial problems, or other conditions may add unbearable stress. With friends there may arise misunderstandings, incompatibilities, or disagreements that cannot be bridged. Finding forgiveness, making accommodations to changed circumstances, or reaching a reasonable compromise may save the relationship, but sometimes a friendly or painful parting is the only solution.

Each one of us is unique and complex. There exists something (or a number of things) within each of my complicated friends that resonates with some part (or parts) of my own multifaceted psyche. Discovering those commonalities or differences and exploring them together provides one of the great delights of friendship. Just as I try to appreciate them in their completeness, I am gratified that my friends see beyond narrow, stereotypical designations, such as "She is just an old woman." Instead, they acknowledge my uniqueness, reflect back to me my more positive qualities, thus reinforcing my better traits. Our conversations make me feel good about myself, and encourage me to further improvement. I am motivated to become the person they imagine me to be. A kind of mirroring goes on, for in our discussions I show my appreciation of those qualities I most admire in them, and by seeing them in the fullness of their unique personhood, I am contributing to their well-being. Thus a reciprocal bond of love and respect is established.

In addition to seeing the distinctiveness, goodness, complexity, and depth in each other, and in developing mutual trust, genuine relationships require time. We must be available to our mates or friends, offer them support, nurture, encouragement, and consolation when needed, which may require extra attention and effort. I have been aware for some years that I must limit the number of friends I have, for I wish to have sufficient time to devote to each one, while protecting my need for solitude. Having a large number of superficial acquaintances is not satisfying in the same way as having a smaller number of faithful friends.

So it is that I find such great pleasure in my current array of relationships. I value the opportunity to share with them my joys and desires as well as my disappointments and worries, and to listen to their equally unique and complicated concerns. I discover and affirm my own wholeness in communion with them. When I stop to reflect, I am awed by the truly amazing people that I count as my friends. I am greatly honored by their presence in my life, for they have enriched me in more ways than I can name. It is their friendship that makes me who I am. Their expressions of love and admiration often surprise, and always comfort and sustain, me. These relationships give me what I think of as *soul nourishment.* It is as if I were an empty vessel, now being filled with sweet water, my thirst for love and respect being tenderly quenched by my fabulous friends.

OCTOBER 2018

Up-LYFT-ing

After a visit with my friend Susanna, who lives in San Francisco, I usually I take a cab to the airport. But on this occasion she suggested calling LYFT, which is convenient and cheaper than a cab. She was told that the car would arrive in about three minutes. When a white car appeared, I opened the door on the passenger side of the front seat, ready to step in. I quickly realized my error. Even with a car service, I would ordinarily sit in the back seat. But as I started to close the door, the young driver beckoned for me to sit in the front. So I did. And with that began an adventure.

My fervent desire now is to have a better memory because I would love to remember the fullness of the conversation I had with that young LYFT driver for our forty-five minute drive to the airport. While I cannot remember the specifics of our exchange, I will always recall the essential sense that this young man, in spite of our age difference, was truly interested in me as a person, was curious about my life. That in itself is unusual, particularly in a situation of this sort.

Our dialogue was not easy, for he spoke with a heavy, unfamiliar accent. I informed him immediately of my hearing loss, which would make it especially difficult to understand him. I frequently asked him to repeat what he had just said and he did so patiently. He never seemed irritated by my failure to understand. He kept asking questions as he expertly wound his way through the heavy traffic. He wanted to know if Susanna was a relative and what she did. He asked me to tell him something about my life and what I did. I told him I had written some books and briefly described my most recent one. He asked if he could buy it on Amazon. When I said it was not available there, he seemed disappointed, so I told him I would mail him one if he would text me his address which he readily agreed to do.

As we drove on, he asked if I had any advice for him. I explained to him that I do not give advice, but hope what I write might give people insight into how they can handle problems similar to mine. He said that he wished I lived in San Francisco for he would like to get to know me better. (How astonishing is that from a twenty-something young man?) I did not wish to pry into his private life, but I did ask where he grew up. He said he is from Yemen and has no family in San Francisco but that there is a large Yemeni community. I observed that he had an impressive English vocabulary. He told me that he likes languages and speaks many, and that he takes lessons in English that are offered at no cost.

I was curious about his immigration status and he told me that he has a green card and in the next few months will be eligible to apply for citizenship. He seemed pleased with the way his case has been handled, and compared it to some relatives in Malaysia, who still have no papers after ten years of residence there. He obviously was very much looking forward to becoming a citizen of the United States.

As we neared the airport I asked his name which he spelled it for me: Yahya. As I got out of the car, Yahya retrieved my bag from the trunk, we shook hands and said goodbye. A little while later I saw that I had missed a phone call with a 415 (San Francisco) area code. I had no idea who it was from, since I knew it was not Susanna's number. A bit later I got another call and it was from Yahya. He just wanted to know that I was okay and had found my gate. I reminded him to send me his address and almost immediately I received it in a text. He also said this, which touched me deeply: *"Knowing you, it'd be the first step to change life better. Please let me know when you get home, just checking in on you."*

So, that is my story. Making friends with a young Yemeni on a ride to the airport. It is a very good feeling to think that I may have had a positive impact on this young man's life. It is something that happens to all of us. Knowingly or not, we have an effect on those with whom we work or otherwise associate. This young man let me know in the kindest way that he felt he had something to learn from an old woman, a stranger in his new country.

DECEMBER 2018

SUPPORT

During a recent yoga class, Mary had each of us choose a word from a collection she passed around. We were then to use that word as a focus for a mindful walking meditation. My word was *support*. I was initially disappointed, for the word did not resonate with me. Support? I can offer support and sometimes need support. What else is there to consider? But after further thought I began to realize that the word has many meanings. For one thing, it can be used as both a verb and a noun. We can support someone or something, and we can also offer or receive support. There are dozens of terms that are synonyms for both the noun and verb forms, each with its own particular nuance and subtlety of meaning. I began to see the word as a richer source of reflection than I had originally thought.

Though I was not thinking of that as I first contemplated the term, one meaning of the word *support* relates to architecture. The foundation, beams, studs, columns, rafters, are all used to support a building. Those words can serve as metaphors for the construction of our personhood. Our family of origin serves as a foundation upon which we shape our later lives. We hope it is firm and sturdy as we assemble skills, knowledge, insights, and understandings that function as strong and durable walls and roof that house our bodies and souls.

Usually I think of support in terms of help. I must admit that at my age (ninety years old) the idea of support is laden with foreboding. At what point will I need substantial care, and how will I acknowledge and accept that? In our culture we greatly value independence and dread the thought of becoming dependent, that is, in need of support. But as I think more deeply, support does not necessarily imply physical care. There are many ways of giving and accepting support.

Support can be financial, as in providing needed funds, but often is non-monetary assistance in the form of collaborating, boosting, sponsoring, or promoting a creative endeavor. Support also comes in the form of emotional sustenance, be it understanding, encouragement, empathy, validation, or merely offering a real or imaginary shoulder to lean on when someone we love is in need of comfort. Humans are social beings, so we search for those relationships that provide whatever kind of support we need most. It may come in the form of a visit to banish loneliness or stimulation to keep our minds alert. A sympathetic listener lends support when we rant and complain. Or it may merely be in the form of a friend or mate with whom we share our troubles and/or joys over a cup of tea or a glass of wine. Support comes in all shapes and sizes.

When thinking of these different kinds of support, I am reminded of an occasion many years ago when my mother-in-law needed help. Her husband had died and she could no longer afford her apartment. My husband Norman and his siblings Al and Jeanette met with a social worker to explore a new living arrangement. I have always admired their solution to support their mother: each would give what they could.

We had an extra bedroom, so she would move in with us. Al had financial resources, so he agreed to help with her expenses. Though they had a smaller home, Jeanette and her family invited her mother to stay with them on many weekends, giving us time and opportunity to pursue our own activities. It was a cooperative, amicable resolution, aided immensely by the adaptive, gracious, and sensitive nature of Norm's Mom, who we called Baba.

This arrangement lasted for several years, with my mother-in-law integrating herself smoothly into our household routine. That is, until one night when Baba, who suffered from heart disease, had an attack while Norm and I were out for dinner. Our young daughters were understandably upset and frightened. Baba, forever the caring and compassionate woman she was, immediately told us that she needed more support. She would move into what was then called The Jewish Old Folks Home, for she did not want to ever again frighten or worry our children in case she had another attack. Her example of acceptance, of adaptability, of concern for our family, has served as a laudable, exemplary attitude for me.

As I have grown into the age group known as the *oldest old*, I readily acknowledge that I am seriously dependent on the emotional support I get from my family and friends. Though not yet in great need of physical care, that time may well soon come when I will be called upon to admit a need for that kind of support. Though our circumstances are different, I aspire to the kind of flexibility and acceptance that Baba displayed, and fervently hope that I can adapt to those changing conditions with graciousness and gratitude.

MARCH 2019

Kindness

In this time when there is so much rudeness, crudeness, and absence of empathy in our culture, especially in social media and from our current president, it helps to remember that kindness is still the most valued of all human responses. I was reminded of that during a recent trip to Mexico. My experience affirms that kindness remains alive, pervasive, and precious.

It began at the St. Louis airport as I prepared to leave for my trip to Oaxaca to visit my granddaughter. I presented my identification, got my ticket, and asked where to check my bag. The agent directed me downstairs, which seemed wrong, but she insisted. Once downstairs I asked directions from a young Black man, an airport employee. He said I needed to go back upstairs and insisted on accompanying me to be sure I found the right place. Once I checked my bag, I sought out the young man to thank him for his help. He said that if I signed a form he might get a bonus from his boss. I was happy to do that. Then, the unexpected! This young Black man reached out and gave me a big hug. What a beautiful gesture of appreciation and kindness. And what a marvelous, heart-opening way to begin my trip.

I had a several hour layover in Houston before my flight to Oaxaca, so I decided to get some lunch. I sat at a table on a long bench of tables for two, a short distance away from a man who was also alone. He asked where I was going. When I replied, he told me he also was going to Oaxaca. We then engaged in a conversation in which he said he had bought property and had decided to retire there after living most of his life in Wyoming. It was a casual, friendly, and somehow affirming, encounter.

After lunch I went to the gate where I would wait for my flight. I explained to the agent that my hearing is such that I might not understand the announcement and wished to be sure not to miss the flight. He said not to worry, that he would come over and inform me personally when the announcement was made—which he did! What an extraordinarily kind and thoughtful thing for him to do.

As I sat waiting for the flight a couple sat down next to me, also obviously going to Oaxaca. They asked about my purpose for the trip so I explained that I have a granddaughter there who runs a creative residency program. They were immediately intrigued, and looked up Pocoapoco on their computers. It so happened that the man runs a similar program in Oregon and hoped to visit Jessie's site while they were in Oaxaca. Quite a synchronicity, and another positive sign that this trip was going well. By then my minor apprehension about traveling alone had completely vanished.

When we arrived at our destination, my newly-made friends—both the man and the couple—were sufficiently concerned about me that they offered to share rides, wanting to be sure that I was well taken care of. Of course, they need not have worried, for Rachel and Jessie were waiting for me with wide smiles and open arms—as I knew they would be. I introduced them to my new friends and then we all parted ways.

My return trip was much the same. Going through customs was tiring and tedious, but I found that whenever I was uncertain about what to do or where to go next, all my questions were answered with courtesy and patience.

The trip taught me lessons, or at least confirmed what I already knew to be true: most people are kind and wish to be helpful. Perhaps the more significant lesson, however, is a reminder to be kind to others. By remembering how much the kindness of others meant to me in what could have been trying situations, I now am more aware of how important it is to show similar openness and kindness to those I come upon in my everyday activities. It is especially important to be kind to those who seem troubled or withdrawn. All of us struggle with sorrows or difficulties at one time or another. Having a gesture or kind word directed our way can be extremely comforting.

At my late age I am still learning from these everyday life experiences. My exchanges with strangers on this recent trip serve as a prompt to keep in mind what is most important in living a fulfilling life. Though I do not think of myself as a religious person, perhaps I can aspire to be like the Dalai Lama when he was asked about his religion. His reply was "My religion is very simple. My religion is kindness."

THE SELF

FEBRUARY 2019

IDENTITY

In the past few weeks I have read two books which, in very different ways, have been of special interest to me. They are about identity: what it is, how it is established, and how we are defined by it. The first is *Inheritance: A Memoir of Genealogy, Paternity, and Love* by Dani Shapiro. In it the author writes movingly about her shocking discovery (when in her fifties) that the father she had grown up believing was her biological father, was not. Due to fertility issues, her parents had resorted to artificial insemination. She had never been told this and was particularly upset because she was very close to her father. Shapiro had been raised in an orthodox Jewish household, her father from an extremely distinguished line of Jewish ancestors. Her biological father, whom she eventually contacted, was Christian.

The other book, much more scholarly in tone and substance, is *The Lies that Bind: Rethinking Identity* by Kwame Anthony Appiah, a philosopher and professor at NYU. You may recognize his name, as I did, as the writer of the Sunday *New York Times Magazine* column *The Ethicist*. It is one of the first things I read in Sunday *Times Magazine*, for I enjoy reading about the ethical dilemmas that are presented and his responses to them.

The kinds of identity addressed in these two books are of different orders. When Shapiro discovers her true biological heritage, she is shaken by what she feels is a tear in the fabric of her personal identity. She felt thoroughly Jewish, had a bat mitzvah, attended Jewish schools, was extremely proud of her distinguished heritage. (By Jewish law, she is Jewish since lineage is determined by the mother.) Throughout her life people had commented that she did not look Jewish; she was blonde, blue-eyed, unlike others in her family. Some of the dissonance she had felt was confirmed by her decided resemblance to her biological father, both physically and in certain gestures and manner of expressions. In very distinctive ways she saw herself mirrored in ways she had not previously experienced.

Appiah, on the other hand, writes about social identity. How do we describe ourselves as part of a group? Is it by gender, nationality, religion, color, culture, class, or a combination of these? Appiah is the son of an English mother and a Ghanaian father so his interest in identity arises from a very personal place. He writes that he is frequently questioned regarding his background, as many people, including taxi drivers, want to know, not just "Where were you born?" (which is London), but more fundamentally, "What are you?". As he delves into each of these categories, he finds endless contradictions, ambiguities, and discrepancies, not only regarding his personal story, but also in general. There is no purity to be found in any of these groupings. One often blends or merges into another.

Different identities, of course, have different expectations, different benefits and responsibilities. In thinking about how the categories of race, nationality, gender, sexual orientation, class, religion, and culture reflect my own identity, I am aware that my personal and social identities, like those of all of us, overlap or intersect. I also realize, but am not surprised, that Appiah does not address age as a category of identity, though I think it is a highly significant one. I most decidedly think of myself—and my culture undoubtedly sees me—as an old white woman. Just as being a woman and being white are socially and personally relevant, so is my age. Like racism and sexism, ageism, as I have noted on other occasions, plays an important role in how the old are perceived and treated in a society that values youthful vigor above all. Those attitudes make one's age an integral part of both personal and social identity.

Labels can be harmful if used in derogatory or destructive manners, but they also matter. Appiah notes that they give us a sense of how we fit into the social world. Identifying myself as "old" gives me permission to behave as my age dictates. I am not held to the physical standards of youth, but can relate to the limitations as well as the advantages of others of my age group. Though at age ninety there is no question about my being old, there is some uncertainty regarding just when that identity becomes applicable. Is it at age sixty, sixty-five, seventy, maybe not even until eighty? There is no definitive answer. The vagueness of where limits lie or definitions apply seems to pertain to almost all the categories. Just as our personal identities are endlessly complex, fading from one into another, so are our social constructs.

Shapiro was understandably confused regarding her personal identity once she found out about her biological heritage. She consulted friends, family members, rabbis, anyone she thought might be helpful. One of the persons offered what he called the three great spiritual questions: *Who am I? Why am I here? How shall I live?*. Many of my reflections have dealt with these queries to some degree. Certainly the first, *Who am I?*, is one I have addressed and continue to ponder. The second, *Why am I here?*, does not feel consequential to me, for I cannot see a meaningful way to address it beyond knowing I am a product of the union of my father and mother. The third, *How shall I live?*, is among the most intriguing and challenging, a question that interconnects with the first. Who I am has tremendous influence on how I live my life. Perhaps the converse is also true: how I live my life determines to a great extent who I am.

The fact is, both our personal and social identities are multifaceted and prone to alterations throughout our life span. How we live our lives is shaped by the many influences we inherit, by the emotional and physical environment in which we live, and by those closest to us. So it seems pertinent to remember that while we learn to respect the multiplicity of both personal and social identities, it is also important to acknowledge that one thing we all share is our humanness. Appiah concludes his book with what is perhaps the most succinct and profound observation regarding that commonality. Written by the Roman dramatist Terence in the second century BCE, it says: *I am human, and I think nothing human is alien to me.*

JANUARY 2019

An Alternative Self

When I was a student at Pacifica Graduate Institute (where I enrolled at age sixty-nine), one of my favorite professors was Christine Downing. She had a deep background in religious studies, depth psychology, and mythology, which she shared in her well-prepared lectures and discussions. Chris also was my dissertation advisor, offering much needed guidance and suggestions for resources. I felt a special bond with her, perhaps because she was close to my age (three years younger). Our personal histories were dissimilar, but I came to see her life as similar to one I might have lived had I been born to different parents and under different circumstances.

Chris was born in 1931 in Leipzig, Germany. Her mother was a pharmacist and a poet, her father, Professor Rosenblatt, taught chemistry at the University of Leipzig. In 1933 he lost his teaching post because the Nazis determined his father was Jewish. The family emigrated to the United States and eventually settled in New Jersey. Chris graduated from Swarthmore with a major in literature and was the first woman to receive a doctorate from Drew University. Her dissertation was on the German philosopher and religious scholar Martin Buber.

She first taught in the Religion Department at Rutgers University, then moved to San Diego State University. That same year she was named the first woman president of the American Academy of Religion and remained in San Diego for eighteen years before moving to Pacifica. There she helped develop the program of Mythological Studies, which was my major. During my matriculation, from 1997-2000, she taught Approaches to Myth, Greek and Roman Mythologies, Mythologies of Monotheistic Traditions, and Goddess Traditions. Later she added courses on memoir and ritual. For her ritual class she is using my book *The Power of Ritual*, which pleases me enormously. This is all to say she has led a very scholarly and academically charged life.

In contrast, I was born in 1928 on a farm in North Carolina. My mother did not graduate high school, though she was proficient at all kinds of handwork, such as sewing, quilting, crochet, and tatting. My father was a farmer, who attended college for one or two years after serving in World War I. He was active in many civic and religious organizations and after I left home was elected to eight terms as state senator. Though undoubtedly fundamentally intelligent, my parents did not place a high value on education or learning, so there was little to no intellectual stimulation in my growing-up years. There were no books in our household other than the Bible.

It was only much later in my life that I began to realize how much I had missed and how hungry I was for knowledge and insight and meaningful discussions. How different my life might have been had I been raised by an educated family, one that had a love of learning, one that introduced me to literature, or encouraged me to pursue higher education. Instead, I was finally able to fully acknowledge, and luckily had the resources to accommodate, my yearning for learning late in my life. Receiving a PhD at age seventy-three was one of the most satisfying achievements of my life.

But I have often wondered what my life might have been like had I had a different upbringing, had my parents, like Chris's, been poets or professors. Perhaps all children (and adults) fantasize about having different parents. None of us is capable of being a perfect fit for our offspring who are of the next generation, and who have their own individual talents, needs, and personalities. I sometimes wonder what my children might have wished for in terms of an ideal mother. I know that in spite of my best efforts I often failed them. I also know that my parents had challenges beyond my understanding and that their limitations were a result of their own particular circumstances. We all do the best we can.

At the same time, fantasies aside, I would not trade the life I have led. Though I might not have had the kind of early intellectual training and encouragement that I longed for, I am grateful to have fulfilled most of my life's few ambitions. In fact, I have accomplished far more than I could have imagined. It is quite possible that had I been brought up under different conditions, I might not have been motivated to develop my own artistic and intellectual gifts. We have no way of knowing what might have been.

What brought on this reflection was a recent exchange of books between Chris and me. I sent her a copy of my *Late-Life Reflections* and she sent me a copy of her latest book (she has written more than a dozen), *Mythopoetic Musings: 2007-2018*. Something she wrote in the introduction of her book brought tears to my eyes, for she expressed so well what I have aimed for in my own more personal musings:

> *In a sense, I realize, they [these essays] are all about me. About how these themes, stories, these mythic figures, these authors—have helped me understand myself. No, more than that. Have helped me become myself. Though I have always hoped they might also be about my students and readers. About you. Might help you know yourself, and those with whom you are intimately connected, and your world more deeply.*

That has certainly been my hope as well. Though my reflections are primarily about me and are a way of helping me "become myself" as Chris puts it, it is also my wish that I might provide you—my family and friends—with insights into your own struggles and in finding your way into meaningful, fulfilling relationships.

JUNE 2019

Chapters

For a while I have been thinking about my long life span as being like a book divided into chapters. Each chapter represents a particular period, some of shorter duration and perhaps less significance than others, but each chronologically following the other. More recently, though, it occurred to me that these chunks of my life might better be thought of as short stories. Each stands alone, each has its own theme, but somehow both fundamentally and tangentially connected, bound together into one volume. Yet another concept that feels even more appropriate is what has been described by the archetypal psychologist James Hillman as "the soul's native polycentricity."

Each of our lives consists of a series of transitions as we move through the stages of childhood, adolescence, mid-life, and old age. It seems to me that for some of us these transitions are more or less smooth—continuous, unbroken, with associations maintained over a lifetime. In contrast, my life feels like a succession of upheavals and separations, divided into distinct segments. It is as if I became a different person as I moved from one place or one stage to the other. The characters in the imaginary short stories or chapters could be seen as various aspects of my one multifaceted self.

Hillman writes that the psyche's basic structure is made up of what he calls *personified images*, another way of saying that we consist of multiple personalities. He describes his own as like a "polytheistic consciousness wandering all over the place, in the vales and along the rivers, in the woods, the sky, and under the earth." Another Jungian author, Andrew Samuels, defines the phenomenon in somewhat different terms: "Psyche brings with it its own plurality, fluidity, and the existence of relatively autonomous entities therein." These entities, he suggests, force us to face "the pluralistic task of reconciling our many internal voices and images of ourselves with our wish and need to feel integrated and speak with one voice."

This notion of multiplicity, or what I often think of as disjointedness within unity, interests me. This construct has a profound resonance with how I have lived my life—for better or worse. As I look back, some transitions, or the emergence of a particular "autonomous entity," felt like a rupture, a tear in the core of my being, shredding a former existence. Perhaps it would be more accurate to say that one of my "personified images" had to die or be suppressed, so that another could be brought to life. Other times the shifts were less dramatic, more gradual, allowing one personification to undergo a smoother blend into another. In the end, of course, all these contribute to the story of my one life, held together by the twisted strands of luck, fortune, or fate.

My sense of disjunction probably began, or certainly was exacerbated, when I ran away from home at age eighteen. That was the first, most severe, most challenging, and most consequential break in my life's story, for it changed the course of the remaining years of my life. I had to leave behind the dutiful Southern daughter in order to give expression to the part of myself demanding independence. All contact with my parents was severed. And it was not just my parents; I had no communication with anyone from my former existence, no siblings, no cousins, no high school friends. Having no one to turn to for advice, I had to depend on my own instincts. Though I had no conscious awareness at the time, I think that original disruption established a pattern of discarding or denying one part of my being in order to allow another to flourish. Later it began to feel natural to move rather abruptly from one way of being to another, starting afresh each time.

During my life span, I have embraced a number of different roles, many which overlapped and each of which added richness to my life. Perhaps the most enduring, across at least seven decades, is my self-identification as homemaker—cook, seamstress, decorator, gardener, manager, and center for my family. Before my children were born, I was director of a preschool for handicapped children and later taught at a school for the deaf. I was, of course, wife, mother, then grandmother and great-grand-mother, all significant identities for me. I was also a photographer, a conductor of rituals, a serious student again in my late years, a caretaker, a widow, and now, a writer. I thoroughly enjoyed each of my many ways of presenting myself and relating to others. You might say I basked in my polycentricity.

I have come to realize that this configuration has both advantages and disadvantages. Due to that drastic disconnection early in my life, I do not feel grounded in my personal history, either of place or of my family of origin. I have had no exchange of ideas and information from those formative years, no one to correct my undoubtedly distorted recollections. I am fully aware that memories are notoriously unreliable. They are filtered through our subsequent experiences; they have been altered by many tellings and re-tellings. Nevertheless, in my case it has been necessary to rely solely on my own recall of how things were. Since I left home due to irreconcilable differences, I can hardly have a balanced perspective. But I have had no one to provide a differing or opposing view, or a comforting and affirming viewpoint of what happened as I was growing up. I have settled on my own story which is probably not always factually correct, but possibly is in some sense psychologically accurate. Those memories are all that I have.

There is also the disadvantage of not having a sense of continuity, no obvious threads that tie together the many components of my life. I should not say no threads, for there certainly was my marriage of almost sixty years which provided an enduring connective cord. There also have been a few connections that have remained, carried over from one phase to another, though none that go back beyond the birth of my children. I formed relationships in each period, but they rarely were sustained once I had moved on—either literally to another place, or psychologically. As my interests changed, a new persona emerged. For example, most of my current friends were unknown to me before my husband's death, more than eleven years ago. They never met the man who exerted so much influence on my life. I am not sure how or why that is true: it is what I have become accustomed to doing. Though in large measure I have made a new life for myself, the few friends that have persisted, especially those that knew Norm, are especially treasured.

There is a potential danger in what may seem like a fragmented life, that of losing touch with the core self, of being without a center, scattered, without cohesion. Being ready to conform to any new situation or convenience poses the risk of abandoning any integrity, of betraying established beliefs and standards. Manifesting a series of personas could feel like not having any mooring, nothing solid to hold on to. For the most part I have been able to avoid that danger. I have largely remained true to myself while responding and adjusting to new surroundings or new situations. I have had the opportunity to react to exterior circumstances or environs with a new attitude or approach while still relying on my own social and psychological center. That centeredness remains firmly within and stands with me wherever I am.

While there certainly are many drawbacks in not having contact with family and friends from my many previous lives, I am aware that moving from one place or one situation to another without restraints has had its advantages. It has given me a fair amount of flexibility and a sense of freedom. At each stage I have been able to re-order my life, regenerate or revitalize myself in order to fit in with new circumstances and new acquaintances. In making new friends and adjusting to different environments, I learned new ways of looking at life, and at myself. Resilience is a worthwhile quality, contributing to openness and allowing for growth.

Another benefit of what has been referred to as the "plural psyche" is that our human personalities offer a plethora of riches: beauty, ugliness, stability, chaos, power, darkness, light, movement, magic, confusion, clarity, messiness, order, humor, thievery, truthfulness, lying, hate, love, and much much more. By acknowledging these pluralities we develop a deeper sense of understanding and tolerance, both for our own vagaries and those of others. We then have a greater appreciation of diversity, especially important in our modern existence.

It occurs to me that these reflections, and especially this one, can be seen as self-indulgent, if not self-centered. Perhaps it is an affliction of old age! But I find great pleasure in looking back and trying to sort out just how my life looks in retrospect. It also makes me even more thankful for living so long. I can readily say that now, in my old age, I do have one strong, unbreakable "tie that binds," and that is my family. No words can adequately express my gratitude for my daughters, their spouses, my grandchildren and their spouses or significant others, and now my great-grandchildren, for their attentiveness and affection. Due to my "soul's native polycentricity," I may have missed out on retaining some connections from the past, but I would not trade any of those for the bonds I have with my loving and lovable family.

The Essential Self

JULY 2019

In my reflection titled *Chapters*, I speculated that all of us have multifaceted psyches, an attribute especially pronounced in my case. But this presents a paradox: while we consist of a variety of personified images or semi-autonomous entities, at the same time each of us is one person, housed in one body, easily identifiable. How do we reconcile these seemingly conflicting perspectives of multiplicity within unity? Since I ventured into the concept of polycentrism, it seems only natural, or fair, that I attempt to define just what makes up the central, cohesive part. I think of this as the essential self. What singular quality or combination of qualities binds together all our varied aspects into one whole?

As we go through the various stages of our lives, we undergo many changes: in our physical bodies, in where we live, in how we subsist, in our relationships, and in how we look at the world. Still, in some sense, we remain the same person we always have been. The poet May Sarton, writing in her seventy-ninth year, addresses this in her book *Endgame*. She says that if someone who had read her books, the last one written seventeen years earlier, came looking for her, she would have to answer that "She did live here but she is not here now." Sarton acknowledges that neither her values nor her way of life have changed in any major way, and yet she asserts, "I am no longer the person who wrote those books." So, she is both the one who has not changed, and also the one who is no longer the person she was. This thought, she says, is depressing; losing her identity as a writer brings her sorrow.

Another woman, the author and Jungian analyst Florida Scott-Maxwell, writing in her eighties, makes a similar observation: "Life has changed me greatly, it has improved me greatly, but it has also left me practically the same." Scott-Maxwell poses the conundrum that though life has improved her greatly, her faults have persisted. She admits, "I still have the vices that I have known and struggled with—well it seems like since birth." She goes on to say that near the end of her life when she is more herself than ever before, she feels "part of a network," that she is "awareness at the mercy of multiplicity." Her contention is that while she is manifold, and has changed in various ways, still there is some inner consistent center, something that leaves her "practically the same."

Like both these women, I have changed in many ways, have greatly improved (though certainly am not without faults), and yet I also feel that some essential part of my being has endured. As I ponder, trying to expose this essential self to myself, I find it impossible to determine just when my basic qualities appeared. We are not born as blank slates, but have embedded in our budding psyches certain propensities, talents, and susceptibilities. So the characteristics that became apparent later may well have been innate or the result of early childhood conditions, but are expressed in different ways as I got older.

As I described in *Chapters*, one result of what I see as my multiplicity is that I have had the tendency to segregate the periods of my life into discreet segments. As a result I have perhaps been too quick to abandon friendships with those who no longer fit with my current interests or outlook. What remains the same is a frequent dissatisfaction with the status quo and a curiosity that has driven me to move on to other relationships and to eagerly embrace new phases of life. For example, the title of my book on aging, *The Unexpected Adventure of Growing Old*, indicates that I view old age, not so much with fear and dread as do so many, but with inquisitiveness and wonder. Sometimes our greatest shortcomings can also be our greatest assets. Leaving behind former attachments and acquaintances, as regretful as that might be, has given me the freedom to explore new pursuits and forge new relationships.

As I mine my own life experiences for insight, it seems that my willingness to explore new territory has depended on a kind of ingrained fearlessness, a boldness that enabled me to seek independence and individuality. I was moved to take chances even though there was no guarantee that the outcome would be entirely beneficial. To ignore obvious peril or to discount warnings of almost certain calamity, is to be reckless in the extreme, but sometimes circumstances become so untenable that a drastic change is necessary. However, for anyone jumping into an unknown future, such as launching an uncertain business or career, developing a new skill, moving to a new town or country, or initiating a new relationship, there must be a willingness to accept the risk of disappointment.

Along with that risk, some amount of (possibly misplaced) courage and confidence, along with a healthy dose of naiveté, is necessary for making major changes. I could not have run away from home, become a photographer, gone back to school at age sixty-nine, or written books, had I not anticipated some degree of success. Nevertheless, I was largely clueless, not fully aware of the likelihood of failure, but also willing to face the possibility of disappointment and defeat. Another way of phrasing this could be that I was (and am) comfortable with uncertainty. Apparently some inner force, some measure of audacity, propelled me forward and my life has been richer for it. (I am reminded of Barack Obama's book *The Audacity of Hope*. Perhaps I had some measure of hope, too.)

Another trait that may be related to hope, and that I feel has contributed to my wellbeing, is that I am fundamentally an optimist. I'm not sure how that happened as I suffered greatly from depression in my early and midlife. But now I tend to focus on the positive, and have an expectation that all will turn out well. I have read that pessimists are more in touch with reality, which may be true, but I prefer to believe that we humans will find a way, though with many missteps, to solve, or at least address, our many challenges.

Perhaps a better term for what I am referring to as the essential self, is "authentic self." I worked with a Jungian analyst for many years when in my sixties. The greatest gift from that time was her gentle guidance in helping me get in touch with my authentic self through exploring my thoughts and examining my dreams. It was journey of self-discovery, learning who I am when not administering to anyone or actively engaged in an occupation. In the beginning of my analysis I could define myself only as a wife, a mother, and a grandmother. It was even hard to think of myself as a photographer, though at the time I had spent a lot of time doing that work. But who was

I when I was not working, or being a parent or grandparent, or being a mate for my husband? It took some time to figure that out, a process that is ongoing. (Otherwise why would I be writing about it now?)

Authenticity is something we readily recognize and admire in people; conversely we abhor people who are insincere or affected. Somehow we can sense if a person is "putting on," merely playing a role, or are projecting a persona reserved only for public appearances; they just seem phony. Unless these identities or personalities are consciously planned and crafted, such individuals are not being true to themselves. They are so focused on their outer lives, or are so profoundly invested in their professional reputations, that they have obliterated access to what is going on inside their hearts and souls. Seeking to be in touch with our innermost selves, or identifying fundamental qualities is not about intellectual knowledge. Rather, it is a desire to be genuine human beings, true to our deepest values, doing our best to live up to the highest standards of honesty, integrity, and just plain decency.

Another way to think of the essential self is as the *being* self as opposed to the *doing* self. It is when we are in touch with the part of ourselves more concerned with being than doing, that we are closer to who we truly are. If we are caught up in too much busyness, working too many hours, or spending too much time on our phones following social media, there is no opportunity for developing and nurturing that part of ourselves that most reveals our true nature. Taking time out to sit quietly in our favorite chair, or take a walk, or a nap, or have a cup of tea or a glass of wine can be restorative.

To access just what it is that lies at the center of our being requires us to develop self-awareness. That awareness, or consciousness, can be acquired over time. It helps us become more cognizant of our behavior, more alert to and more mindful of what we do and say. It also helps us feel an inner alignment, allowing us to be more comfortable in our own skin. In my earlier life I often made decisions without any clear understanding of the impact those decisions might have. As I have grown older, I still make mistakes, sometimes say something tactless or hurtful, or do something foolish, but I have become more aware of those missteps, and, I hope, am now more conscious, more thoughtful, more reflective. It is a sign of maturity, I think, when we learn to depend on our *essential, authentic,* or *being* self for guidance, and can acknowledge when we have betrayed that self.

Not being in touch with that core part of ourselves can cause immense pain, especially as we get older. Persons who have largely depended on their professions, or their positions, or in the case of women who depended on their beauty or their youthfulness can suffer greatly when those individualities or qualities are no longer present to bolster their sense of self. Without those formerly identifying statuses or functions or looks, they can feel lost and depressed. Something else is then required to satisfy a meaningful existence.

So it is advisable to pay attention, to make an effort to develop greater awareness of that authentic self. It is not always an easy process. At age ninety I am still working on being true to my inner self. The questions arise, How do we determine if we are being true to ourselves? Who is the judge? I rely on my "observer self," some facet or attribute of my mind that seems to be looking at my behavior and my beliefs. While not exactly fiercely judgmental, this "observer" nevertheless lets me know if something I say or do does not comport with my ethical standards by arousing in me a sense of unease or regret. It is when I feel most centered, calm, and content that I can be reasonably certain that I am connected to my essential self. It is then that I feel I am living into my strengths, that I am being true to that part of myself that represents the best that I can be.

It is my experience that we become more interested in these questions as we grow old. We become more introspective, more inner-focused. Certainly that is true for me. When we are young or in midlife, the everyday demands of building a career, making a living, or raising a family require most of our attention. As we age and have fewer pressures, it is possible to look back and contemplate these basic questions regarding how we live our lives. Having abundant times of solitude and silence, another advantage of advanced age, is most beneficial in helping us stay in touch with that inner, essential self. I am greatly blessed to have those advantages and to have lived long enough to share these thoughts with all of you.

AUGUST 2019

A Theme Revisited

Last month I wrote two reflections (Chapters and The Essential Self) that dealt with my sense of being both fragmented and yet unified. As I indicated, my life has consisted of a series of distinct periods that I called chapters, and yet, like all of us, I have an essential self that transcends or incorporates all of those disparate experiences and stages of life. Recently, in looking through some files on my computer, I found an essay I wrote ten years ago (2009) that deals with a comparable paradox, though I approached it from the perspective of aging. Now that I will soon be ninety-one, I thought it might be interesting to see how I viewed this topic a decade earlier, as I was entering my eighties. So, with a few editing changes, here it is.

There is a widely held belief that the longer we live, the more we become who we are. One woman, writing in her eighties, says, "I am myself as never before." Though the body may lose physical endurance and flexibility with increased age, the inner self, the essence of who we are, continues to maintain its strength, perhaps even grows in vigor, over our lifetime. According to this perspective, there exists within each of us some imprint that was there from the beginning, something like an acorn that has encoded within it a guide necessary to produce an oak tree.

Just as the majesty of the oak emerges from within the tiny acorn, or as the sap rises within the tree to promote its growth, so there is within each of us some inner push that propels us onto our natural path. It is the life force that urges us onward, that pulls us toward our personal fulfillment, and that connects and coordinates our inner pluralities. It forms our character, and it takes time to fully ripen. When we are old we have more time to think about those characteristics that contribute to our individuality, and how we have melded them together to form that central character. We may find value, not just in our conformities which have been readily accepted, but also in our oddities which may have been scorned, seeing both as manifestations of our integrity and demonstrations of our beliefs. As we live out the extent of our years, we are slowly unfolding, drawing upon our inner resources and potentialities and reinforcing the patterns that make up our personality and define our character.

Those of us who have lived enough years begin to see some of the elements that make up our life stories and can sometimes catch glimpses of the interior structures that are displayed in our complex personalities. The acorn may have a singular purpose in becoming an oak tree, but the oak tree has many possible variations in its history of growth, depending on—among other things—environment, climate, and exposure to pests and disease. Just so, our social, cultural, and educational influences, our experiences of positive and/or negative personal interactions, and our exposure to a variety of opinions and beliefs shape the basic biological and psychic material with which we are born.

No other person has had exactly our combination of inherited features and specific experiences. Each of us accumulates a peculiar combination of disappointments and achievements, vices and virtues, cruelties and kindnesses, and it takes time to merge these often disparate, sometimes contradictory, qualities into a more or less cohesive whole, a unity which represents our fundamental character. Our uniqueness is something to be embraced and celebrated, especially as we grow old. A famous quote by Martha Graham is worth repeating: "There is a vitality, a life force that is translated through you into action. And because there is only one of you in all time, this expression is unique, and if you block it, it will never exist through any other medium and will be lost." Graham insists that we owe it to ourselves and to posterity to express our distinctiveness in whatever way is open to us. Another writer put it this way: "When life's vicissitudes seem too much to bear, it is worth remembering just how amazing each of us really is."

To switch metaphors, it seems that when we come into this world we already have emblazoned on the canvas of our beings a rough draft of who we are and what we will become. We remain true to that stamp of identity regardless of our subsequent experiences; in fact all our experiences are influenced, even molded, by that original contour. In our later years we have come to terms with that essence; we have learned to accept our weaknesses and failures and can acknowledge our strengths and successes. The awareness of our unique complexity, with its particular combination of good and bad features, fosters a deeper appreciation of our individuality; we have a clearer vision of ourselves as distinct, differing in significant ways from those around us. We may cease to be embarrassed by our eccentricities and instead delight in an image of ourselves as unconventional, even weird. We are finally able to fully express and embrace our character, that which makes us who we are.

The paradox is, that though we continue to grow and learn, we also remain the same. As so many of us have found, part of that continuing development and learning is in acknowledging those innermost characteristics that we so often decried, denied, and denigrated when we were younger and were still striving to present ourselves as unflappable, infallible, and invulnerable. In our old age we learn to be comfortable with our failures, knowing full well that none of us is without them. One old man gives his views on positive aging by comparing it to whiskey. "Old whiskey is just more interesting than young, green whiskey. … It has time to take on all that character of the wood." Like whiskey in a barrel, growing old adds to the fullness and flavor of human life. Aging offers us the opportunity to soften some of our youthful roughness, to sprinkle in some savory seasoning, and thereby contribute to a richer and more rewarding character.

Most of us, regardless of age, are aware of a continuity of self, an agelessness, as if we have always been this same person, even though our appearance and our circumstances may have changed dramatically over the years. And yet, paradoxically, though we retain a strong sense of unaltered identity, of individuality, we can and do transform into different, and, it is hoped, more mature versions of ourselves.

It is those possibilities, those expressions of our individuality, those reactions to the wide range of experiences endured or enjoyed by us, that reveal our character. Though our bodies may weaken and our memories fade, our character is strengthened as we age, for it is not dependent upon physical agility or outer appearance, but rather is a manifestation of the continued growth of our uniqueness. The inner core of our being is reinforced rather than diminished as we grow old, and it is the knowledge of that continued development that sustains us and can make our later years fruitful and meaningful.

Though I have retained a strong sense of "me-ness," I feel I am a profoundly different person than I was in my younger years, and not just in the way I look. As I enter my eighties, I feel a softening of my edges, a blurring of formerly rigidly held beliefs, an ability to see gradations of gray between the extremes of blacks and whites, a yielding of harsh judgments to more compassionate understanding. This is not to say that I no longer hold firm opinions, or that I have ceased to see the brilliant colors and intriguing shapes of the world around me, or that I now fail to be incensed by injustice and violence. I do not feel that I have become a paler version of my former self, diminished by my age, but rather that I have taken on more complexity, developed more nuance, enlarged my landscape of ideas, and that makes for a fuller, more variegated, and less sharp-edged personality. To introduce yet another metaphor, perhaps the addition of years of life experience allows for an interweaving of all aspects of the self, thus blending the threads of anger and disappointment and sorrow in with the brighter, cheerier colors of love and joy and acceptance, producing a more balanced and more satisfying life-tapestry.

There is not much I would add to this reflection written a decade ago. I continue to aspire to "enlarge my landscape of ideas" and to remain grateful for the amazing life I have been given.

The Stories We Tell Ourselves

MAY 2018

Not long ago I was surprised to learn that I could resume tasks that I thought were forever beyond my ability. My arthritic knees were painful, so, quite naturally, I began limiting my movements to avoid discomfort. Even after I had both knees replaced, the months of recovery required me to refrain from too much walking or strenuous activity. I had not appreciated how much my daily activities had been reduced until I became aware of how they have recently expanded. I then began to understand that these decisions about what I could or could not do were due largely to the stories I was telling myself.

Narrative psychology is a recognized field of study which investigates how we create stories in order to make sense of our experiences. Our personal tales give meaning and help provide a sense of purpose as we attempt to integrate the facts and events of our lives. We construct our narratives, repeat them to ourselves, become convinced of their truth, and then proceed to live into the stories, regardless of their accuracy or benefit. According to psychologists who have researched this subject, it is not logic and rationality, but our stories that primarily influence our behavior and upon which we form our identity. They serve as a kind of guidebook to determine which actions we take, or which we seek to avoid. In other words, the stories we tell ourselves, whether we are consciously aware of them or not, have a huge impact on who we are and how we live our lives.

For example, if we tell ourselves that we were wronged, either by poverty, or neglect, or abuse, or by our own misguided behavior, and if we are able to see only that aspect of ourselves, we become victims, weak and defenseless. If we allow such an account to become the overpowering source of our identity, it can disempower us and deny us the courage or capacity to rise above those difficulties and take charge of our lives. But if we can acknowledge the truth of the challenges we faced and yet refuse to buy into the statement that "I cannot succeed because I was mistreated," then we have freed ourselves. We can form another story that will allow us to forge a more positive self-identity. "I know I can succeed in spite of what happened to me."

In certain ways victimhood was one of my stories. I had a troubled, difficult mother, and for a long time I felt victimized by my early painful experiences. Instead of taking responsibility for my attitudes (especially my depression), I initially blamed her for my problems. I finally discovered that though my early life may have been tough, I could, as an adult, benefit by taking responsibility for my own behavior. I learned that I could construct a new narrative, one in which I could acknowledge my past, but not be defined by it. I could create a more hopeful and more helpful way of looking at myself and thus grow into a better, healthier, more balanced person.

I do not mean to over-simplify the process of psychological development or deny the importance of personal or societal influences; our personalities are complex, our thought processes are complicated, and our experiences often present severe hindrances to our progress and welfare. There are many factors that contribute to our mental health. But if we persist in seeing ourselves only through the lens of deprivation or deficiency without a counter narrative that offers the possibility of overcoming those circumstances, then we have fallen prey to an outlook that is detrimental to our growth.

My current stories relate largely to old age. In hopes of making this most interesting time of life as fulfilling as possible, I try to gracefully accept my limitations. I also try not to be unduly influenced by the negative stereotypical attitudes regarding old age so prevalent in our society. I wish to remain realistic about what I can or cannot do while not succumbing to misguided perceptions of my capabilities. Am I truly disabled or am I using my advanced age (almost ninety) as an excuse? Sometimes it is hard to figure out! I monitor the stories I tell myself, so I can better determine if they are still relevant and accurate descriptions of my present physical and mental states or if they are outdated, no longer representative of my true status.

During those years of discomfort due to my knees, for example, I (correctly) told myself I couldn't work in my garden since that kind of work was too stressful for my knees. But this spring I discovered that this story is no longer valid, that with some modifications, I can still plant annuals, clean out my little pond, and do simple maintenance work. I had also told myself I could not travel as I did earlier, fearing the challenges of having to walk long distances from plane to taxi or pickup places. Again I have discarded this story, learned that by using a wheelchair when necessary, or giving myself additional time, I can mostly travel when and where I wish. I also told myself, again correctly, that it is not wise for me to drive at night, but instead of avoiding all nighttime activities, I have learned to use Uber. I am learning to examine my stories and to change them when indicated.

As in my situation, when we experience illness or pain (or old age), we quite naturally begin to adjust to our situation, finding ways to modify our behavior in order to lessen as much discomfort as possible. Even in less extreme circumstances we often unconsciously make subtle changes that tend to limit our activities. In doing so, however, I have begun to realize, we might be doing ourselves a disservice. I find that it is a good idea to challenge myself, to tolerate a moderate amount of pain or fatigue in order to accomplish tasks that I could formerly accomplish with ease. I may take longer, not be quite as efficient, but there is satisfaction in still remaining as active as possible.

Our internalized stories regarding psychological or emotional distress also need to be examined. How do I justify my anger, hopelessness, or sorrow? Could another narrative help alleviate some of my stress and concerns? Could I disengage from those negative moods by formulating another perspective when they begin to overwhelm me? I find it helpful to continually scrutinize my feelings and emotions in order to determine whether they are legitimate considering my current circumstances, or whether they are old patterns, no longer pertinent.

By assessing more of my narratives and adjusting them when indicated, I can alter my conduct and beliefs, arriving at a more realistic understanding and acceptance of both my limitations and possibilities. Perhaps those of you still in the early stages of your lives can benefit from examining your own stories. First of all, do you know what they are and can you put them into words? If so, are they constructive or are they holding you back? Are the stories still appropriate? Can you create alternative ones that might be more advantageous? Can you change the story about the kind of person you believe you are? I would say that it behooves all of us to be aware of, and to be wary of, the stories we tell ourselves, for, as I have found, they may be limiting rather than expanding our possibilities.

APRIL 2018

Daily Challenges

May I live this day
Compassionate of heart,
Clear in word,
Gracious in awareness,
Courageous in thought,
Generous in love.

I have had this poem by the Irish poet and priest John O'Donohue posted on my desk for many years so that I might read it each morning as a blessing for beginning my day. Actually I find myself reading it several times a day since I am at my desk frequently, paying bills, reading and sending emails, working on a writing project.

I like some of his directives, but am confused by others. The first, "Compassionate of heart," is easily understood and to be expected. Compassion is one of those widely admired and frequently touted qualities desired by those of us wishing to live a life based on ethical principles. It is, however, easier to comprehend than it is to apply. I am not at all certain how compassionate I can be towards those that I find disagreeable or who fail to comply with my notion of fairness, justice, and tolerance. But I continue to strive for a deeper level of compassion.

To be "Clear in word" is something I work towards as I write my occasional essays. I wish to express myself with as much clarity as possible, and at the same time reflect my views with as much honesty as I can possibly unearth from the deepest part of my psyche. It is not always effortless, but at least I understand what it is I am attempting.

But when it comes to "Gracious in awareness," I am a bit stumped. What does that mean? Somehow the two concepts do not readily mesh in my mind. Though I try to be gracious—that is, courteous, kind, affable, hospitable, tender—and to develop my awareness—that is, to be conscious, mindful, alert, cognizant, understanding—I struggle to find the essential connection between graciousness and awareness. I posed the question to my friend Sara who said that the image that came to her was "a calm acceptance and graceful attitude and action toward whatever enters our awareness, with an implication of dignity, generosity and ease." Her image (and her language) is inspiring, for graciousness does imply "a calm acceptance and graceful attitude and action." If we can maintain that demeanor as we become aware of some of our more undesirable traits or as we confront unpleasant events that we must withstand, and can do so with "dignity, generosity and ease," then we certainly have come a long way in our psychological and spiritual development. I still am not clear what O'Donohue meant with his curious phrase, but I shall continue to think about it; perhaps that is enough to have served a worthwhile purpose.

Then there is "Courageous in thought." This is hard, for it suggests having the courage to give up comfortable attitudes and beliefs and to think the unthinkable. Because my liberal political views are so entrenched, I find it incredibly difficult to think as a more conservative person might. As a woman belonging to no traditional religion, I find it impossible to think in terms of unquestioned devotion to a particular text or to a single institution as do fundamentalists of all stripes. Though I try to be open to the ideas and thoughts of others, I must reluctantly admit that I am not as courageous in my thinking as I would like. It occurs to me however, that admitting one's lack of courage requires a certain amount of courage. "Generous in love." This one I really get. I know what it means: to be open-hearted, bighearted, to offer love unstintingly and unconditionally, to embrace with open arms all those with whom we come in contact. It means to give love freely, openly, to not be withholding or judgmental. To be generous in love is to reap the rewards of friendship and the closeness of family. It is a formidable challenge to always remember to follow this advice. There are times when I feel vulnerable or afraid, wishing to protect myself from real or imagined pain or rejection. But if I can hold on to it each day, my life will be enormously enriched. For in being generous in love I find that I am then loved generously by others. What could be better than that?

MARCH 2019
Observing, Discerning, Judging

A few weeks ago a friend suggested that I be in touch with a woman that he knew. I was not terribly enthusiastic about the idea, but I agreed. We emailed briefly and she said she would send me some of her books. I agreed to send her some of mine. I was shocked when I got her books. I learned that she is the founder and CEO of an extremely successful international company devoted to training and guiding human resources executives and corporate managers. Her books focused on career development systems, "rethinking career mobility," and ways to foster helpful career conversations with employees. Since I have never had a career, and have never been part of a corporate structure, I could not imagine what we might have in common.

We've all heard of the term "passing judgment." That is exactly what I did. I became irritated at the thought of having to interact with this woman, whom I summarily dismissed as someone entirely out of my league, someone who could not possibly be interested in my very personal book on aging and my reflections on growing old. I dreaded our telephone conversation, which was arranged through her executive assistant. She sent me a digital calendar with day and time duly noted which also put me off since I have never used one. (I am embarrassed to confess, in my admittedly old-fashioned way, I still rely on my desk calendar on which I write my appointments.)

The day came, and surprise! We had an interesting conversation. I learned that she sold her business a few years ago, and, following a period of depression, now at age 75, she is learning how to deal with this later period of her life. Our mutual friend must have told her that I had gone back to school late in life and that I had remained relatively active. She still travels and gives lectures on her specialty, and said that she hopes to come to St. Louis where she would visit and "sit at my knee" to learn more about aging. So much for my hasty judgment.

This incident made me stop and think about how mistaken I was to jump to conclusions about someone I had never met and knew very little about. It also made me want to examine the whole matter of judgment. There are a number of reasons that might prompt any of us to make snap (often negative) judgments. One is a feeling of insecurity or low self-esteem. Was I feeling defensive about not having had a career? Was I projecting onto others qualities difficult to accept in myself, like worrying if I sometimes come on too strong?

Another reason can be that those who routinely form negative opinions of others lack empathy and an inability to recognize the complexity of all us humans. Such persons frequently exhibit entrenched prejudices regarding color, or religion, or political persuasion. Additional causes for impulsive negativity are emotional wounds within ourselves. When they go unrecognized, unresolved, or unhealed, these hurts can lead to anger, resentment, and undeserved hostility toward others.

Tara Brach, a well-known psychologist and meditation teacher, suggests a number of ways that might help us become less judgmental. One is to be mindful, to pause and think before we speak or send that email, that we try to rephrase or reframe our thoughts into something less damaging, more neutral. Another suggestion is not to take comments too personally, to acknowledge that the other person may be dealing with problems unbeknownst to us. The woman I mentioned, seemingly successful in every way, may well be struggling with issues of identity and aging. If we can look for the basic goodness and fundamental humanness in others, even when it is difficult to find, then we are less likely to be overly judgmental.

As unfortunate, mistaken, or misinformed our judgments can be, informed judgment is an essential quality if we are to successfully navigate this world. It is an important skill to develop because having poor judgment can be just as detrimental as being too precipitous in judging. We need to be aware of potential pitfalls and dangers in some situations and respond with appropriate caution or avoidance. The same is true of individuals. We normally assess the people we meet, determine who seems friendly or who appears hostile, and react accordingly. In forming long-term relationships we judge who we can trust and who we cannot, who is capable of love and compassion and who might show signs of lack of empathy or betrayal. Our behavior should be based on sufficient, reliable information. It is when we automatically become suspicious or antagonistic without having ascertained the facts or reality of the situation that our reactions become problematic.

Reflecting on my misguided instantaneous response to a perfectly friendly overture that I described earlier, I would have been better served by first *observing*—paying attention to how little information I had, then thoughtfully *discerning* my willingness to engage with someone new, and only finally, when I had learned more about the reason for this woman's perfectly innocent and gracious interest, should I have moved into the *judging* mode. Instead of doing that, I had it backwards—judging first, rather than last. I hope to do better in the future.

Generosity

SEPTEMBER 2020

Though not among the extremely wealthy, I am fortunate in being comfortably well-off. My situation offers me enormous freedom but also poses challenges regarding how best to use the money I have available. How generous should I be? And to which causes? I struggle with those decisions, for there are many organizations, whether social, political, or cultural, that are equally worthy. I am torn about where my priorities lie, whether I should focus my support in one category more than another since I am interested in all of them.

I wish to be prudent in my disbursements, for it is my desire to reserve as much of my estate as I can for my family upon my death. But the world they will inherit depends in part on the success of institutions and groups that promulgate and protect the moral and ethical principles essential for the preservation of our society. We need to support organizations that recognize the fundamental worth of all persons regardless of color, class, religion, or national origin. I am immensely proud that two such nonprofit organizations (*Nest* and *Doing Good Together*) were founded by members of my family, and I am pleased to support them. All such groups need plentiful funding to carry on their work.

There is also the matter of how generous to be on an everyday level. What percentage to tip waiters or others who provide service? How much to leave for the woman who vacuums our hotel rooms? What to offer for a particularly helpful errand run by a friend? What constitutes a fair wage for those who clean our homes? These decisions are often left to personal discretion, so it behooves us to think carefully about our level of giving.

My dear friend Sara, who follows a Buddhist practice, has given serious thought to what she calls "reciprocal donation." Sara and I have been friends for forty years and she has edited all my prior books. Her health is such that she could not commit to this one, but we remain in close contact and I continue to send her all my reflections. With her permission I am privileged to share with you her eloquent and moving perspective on generosity.

HOW RECIPROCAL DONATION FOSTERS SPIRITUAL AWARENESS

Often expressed as the virtue "generosity," giving—as opposed to payment—is common to many if not all religions. In Buddhist practice, there is no charge for teachings, and students are encouraged to determine for themselves an appropriate amount to give. That amount reflects the value of what they receive from a teacher, their desire to support the teaching so that others may benefit from it, and their circumstances at the time.

Taking those (and possibly other) factors into account, it is impossible to name a flat fee that applies to everyone all the time. Instead, there is the challenge of discerning what donation is right for each of us in each situation. By turning attention inward and allowing time to reflect, we can sense two limits: an amount below which we would feel ashamed and an amount above which we would feel resentful. The right amount falls in the middle. Since that amount is unlikely to be the same for another time, place, and situation, the process is repeated often. Such reflection requires time, but the resulting sense of "rightness," with no second-guessing or leftover emotions, produces satisfaction that we have reached clarity within ourselves and that our contribution is appropriate.

In Judaism, giving (tzedakah) is often viewed in a similarly thoughtful manner, as a middle path between apathy and self-impoverishment. A Jewish practice that can be powerfully heart-opening is setting money aside (ideally, in a special container) whenever we are moved by happiness or by loss, when we feel especially grateful or connected to some aspect of life. Then, when an occasion arises that moves us to express our gratitude, we do so spontaneously by giving money from that fund to someone who needs it or to some cause we want to support.

In both these practices, the act of giving deepens our awareness of our interrelatedness, as we connect our own inner experience with the world around us. Even at the level of ordinary friendships, each simply gives what she has to offer.

Nature itself operates on a "donation" basis rather than direct exchange. A plant is given life through a complex cycle in which soil, atmosphere, animals, chemical actions, human effort, etc., contribute to the plant's growth at various stages, and each of those elements in turn receives what it needs (though with no guarantees). That model allows us to give freely what we have to give, trusting that our needs will be met in the natural course of our interconnectedness. In fostering awareness of the great cycle of giving and receiving, the generosity of life can inspire generosity in us.

—Sara Jenkins

Sara gives us a refreshing way of looking at generosity and provides us with some helpful guidelines to help determine the "right" amount to pay in a variety of circumstances. It may not always be easy to find that middle spot between embarrassment for being too stingy or regret for seeming overly lavish, but a thoughtful inner search can teach us something important about our values. The concept of reciprocal donation has been especially helpful for me as I have used it with some of my friends. We have different life circumstances and therefore bring different offerings which we share without any concern about monetary equivalence. This usually unspoken but mutually accepted understanding helps avoid awkwardness and instead offers meaningful, soul-satisfying exchanges.

Sara also brings to our attention the complexity of giving and receiving that exists in the natural world, reminding us of our ultimate interconnectedness and our responsibilities for one another and for our environment. May we freely give whatever we have to give and graciously receive that which we need. May we always be generous in heart for all peoples and for our endangered earth.

Aging

AUGUST 2018

Newly Ninety

Now that I have turned ninety, I feel like a snake that has recently shed its skin. As I contemplate my newly revealed self, I am filled with curiosity regarding just what unexpected adventures lie ahead of me as one of the *oldest old*, preparing for my tenth decade upon this earth. At the moment it seems thrilling, though I know that I am likely to encounter challenges. Most of us in this age group eventually face some illness or serious disability. If and when that happens to me, I hope I can endure whatever comes with equanimity. Perhaps I should take a lesson from my great-grandson Noah who finds a stoic attitude to be helpful.

It is interesting to think back over the many eras of my life. The older I get the more layers seem to be stripped away. Again, like the snake shedding skin, I feel that I am now getting down to my essential self, having discarded some of my more fraudulent aspects, becoming more authentic and honest, less fearful and uncertain. Fraudulent is not quite the right word; it is too extreme. My younger guises were not consciously false or purposely deceitful. Better to say that the former "skins" served a useful purpose in being protective of an insecure and undeveloped self. Those semblances served a worthwhile purpose in that I have been allowed time and opportunity to learn and grow. Now, however, I feel increasingly genuine in ways I have not experienced before. This new stage of life is both exhilarating and liberating. I am free, ready to move into the beyond without any major encumbrances—whatever that unknown "beyond" may be.

Another way I think of the stages of life is the image of a spiral. Most people think of growing old as a downward spiral; we start out at the top and everything afterwards is downhill. But I see life as an upward spiral. In my view we emerge from our foundation, our family of origin, and then begin our climb. It is not a direct path. We grow from our childhood fantasies, into adolescent anguish, then become striving young adults. Perhaps we turn out to be competent and satisfied adults, maybe parents and grandparents—even fulfilled great-grandparents, like me. We circle around, often repeating old patterns. But each ascending curve of the spiral augments the one below, adding experiences and knowledge and insight. Old habits are altered, new attitudes adopted, maybe a bit of wisdom accrues. So, one hopes, at the summit there will be an enormous uplift—a blast that sends us into whatever may exist in the afterlife—assuming there is such a thing.

At my age I find both these images—the snake shedding its skin and the rising spiral— enormously comforting. I truly feel I am entering this latest stage of life with a new skin of sorts, and I also have a sense of approaching a high point in my life, ready for the lift-off. It has been quite a ride!

NOVEMBER 2019

Aging and Attitude

In the November 4, 2019 issue of *The New Yorker* there was a lengthy article by Arthur Krystal, titled "Why We Can't Tell the Truth About Aging." Krystal reviewed much of the current and past literature on aging, which attempts, in his words, to put "the best face on it that we possibly can. Our senior years are evidently a time to celebrate ourselves and the wonderful things to come: travelling, volunteering, canoodling, acquiring new skills, and so on. No one, it seems wants to disparage old age." He then proceeds to do just that. He belittles these accounts of "wonderful things," by quoting the comedian Rodney Dangerfield who, he believes, said it best: "I'm at the age where food has taken the place of sex in my life. In fact, I've just had a mirror put over the kitchen table."

While Krystal acknowledges studies that have found that people's sense of well-being was highest in childhood and old age, with a perceptible dip around midlife, he is skeptical of their validity. He suggests, without any evidence, that "the people who participate in such studies are those whose lives tend to follow the curve, while people who feel miserable at seventy or eighty, whose ennui is offset only by brooding over unrealized expectations, don't even bother to open such questionnaires."

His cynicism is further advanced by his perusal of medical literature which focuses on the shortening of telomeres, whose length is a measure of cellular health. As he declares, there may be a chance that you will be happier at eighty than you were at twenty or forty, "but you're going to feel much worse." He insists that "the optimistic narrative of pro-aging writers doesn't line up with the dark story told by the human body." He points out that sixty-eight per cent of Medicare beneficiaries today have multiple chronic conditions. He then adds, sardonically, "Not a lot of grace, force, or fascination in that."

Krystal demeans those who insist that life doesn't necessarily get worse after seventy or eighty. He insists that "it does, you know. I don't care how many seniors are loosening their bedsprings every night; something is missing." He seems to equate perhaps his own failing sexual prowess with a meaningless old age, wondering "Who the hell wants to tear his or her clothes off at seventy-five?" He claims that he doesn't care that he may not have much to contribute after he is seventy-five. Really! I suppose if lively sexual activity is his only measure of a satisfying old age, perhaps he is right, but I find it sad that at age seventy-one Arthur Krystal has resigned himself to a future of loss and decline and hopelessness. As a writer, surely he still has much to offer. I fear that he will live into his predictions, thus squandering the years he has left.

I would argue that much of Krystal's analysis is based on the kind of pessimistic attitude towards aging that is all too prevalent in our culture. He seems to have fallen prey to what Margaret Gullette, professor and author of books on ageism, calls "America's decline-oriented culture." At Krystal's age, I was in graduate school, looking forward to one of the most rewarding and productive—and happiest—periods of my life. Widowed at age eighty, never having written before, I wrote four books in the following decade. I am not alone in my late-life productivity, for I have many friends who have continued to be creative in their seventies, eighties, and nineties.

After talking about my reactions to this article with some friends, I found that some do not share my views. One disavowal came from my physician son-in-law, Dan, who reminded me that many persons in their sixties, seventies, and eighties are undergoing serious medical issues. These ailments may make it difficult for them to see life through the rather optimistic lens that I suggested. He is absolutely right. Another response came from a former classmate with whom I shared my outrage, since I thought he might enjoy my thoughts on what Krystal had to say about old age. I received his commentary, which, with his permission, I include here.

I have been mulling over Leah's thoughts on the Krystal article since it is quite germane to my own engagement with aging, disability and meaning. The challenge to the dilemma of aging seems to be beyond a binary choice of boon or bane.

The later years afford for some, who are not in a subsistent struggle for existence (e.g. the homeless), a time for leisure and reflection. Personally, I have been given this opportunity beyond that which most others have not. I am not wealthy, but I am well-to-do; I do not have to scrabble to live. And, it is likely that I am blessed by not being extraordinarily wealthy since great wealth often seems to possess the possessor.

On the other hand, I awaken every morning to the specter of physical diminishment. Where I formerly moved with ease about the house, I now awkwardly lurch about at the edge of falling. I still attend an exercise class several times a week, only to be reminded of my failing balance and movement. At these times, I could succumb to the sentiment contained in the statement by Arthur Krystal that "the optimistic narrative of pro-aging writers doesn't line up with the dark story told by the human body." Krystal holds that aging is much more bane than boon. Perhaps here, a cultural context might be considered.

It seems to me that our culture has a bias to focus on, and to favor, the exoteric over the esoteric; what is manifest is more important than that which is subtle. We value a "selfie" over a reflective thought.

I first experienced neuropathy in my fifties during a time that I was writing my dissertation. For decades, I had been a habitual runner. At this point with the onset of neuropathy, I was slowed from a run to a walk. And, in that slowing, I saw what I previously had sped by. I saw in a coastal estuary a metaphor for a subtle heart – and that insight changed everything for me.

So now in my late seventies, as I am tempted to despair over the "dark story" of my bodily decline, I remember the epiphany at San Elijo Lagoon, and of the notion that a wound has a mouth. Perhaps, the wounding of neuropathy is a calling to search for the gold in the dross of decline. In the dark tailings of our lives, there are specks of hidden gold. The meaning in old age may be found in the alchemical mining of those tailings.

—Denis Langhans

Denis's rejoinder gives me pause. I feel embarrassed and greatly humbled. I am extremely fortunate, especially at age ninety-one, to still be both well-off and in good health. There is no question that my comfortable life and my physical well-being contribute greatly to my ability to maintain a positive outlook on aging. It is inestimably more difficult to remain optimistic when suffering from physical diminishment similar to what my friend is experiencing. My lack of sensitivity to that reality, and my failure to adequately address the fact that many others do not share my good fortune, makes it imperative that I face my own arrogance and obliviousness to the situations of others. I am loath to admit these shortcomings, but there it is.

Despite my admitted oversight or insensitivity, I do not feel Arthur Krystal is absolved of responsibility for his negativity towards growing old. At seventy-one, he does not claim any physical disabilities, nor is he among the poverty-stricken. His mind is certainly sharp, as he continues to write for a major publication. Frankly, I see no excuse for his personal pessimism regarding aging. While I own my lack of appropriate sensitivity to the inevitable decline of our aging bodies, I nevertheless abhor the ageism that I see as being all too common in our culture. This ageism is furthered by attitudes such as those espoused by Krystal.

Denis wrote eloquently about the epiphany he experienced when he had to slow from running to walking. Now he is undergoing yet another slowing and, to his great credit, is searching for "the gold in the dross of decline." That is my wish and my hope for all of us who are aging. I hope that we can find a way to honor that "hidden gold," even in the midst of the inevitable decline and discomforts of our old bodies and minds.

SEPTEMBER 2019

Letting Go

One of the primary challenges facing us in old age is the necessity to let go of former expectations, activities, and attitudes. It is not an easy process. We must make minor adjustments as well as major ones in the way we live our lives. We have left or retired from our careers. Our families are grown and dispersed. Perhaps our spouse or partner has died. We no longer have the kind of contacts with friends that once meant so much to us. In addition our bodies are going through major changes, such as hearing loss, stiff and painful joints, reduced energy, or diminished mobility. Some of us have endured serious illness that leaves us less than fully functional. Though we prefer to stay in our homes, we may have to move to an independent living center or one with assisted care. We may begin to wonder just who we are, as our very identity feels threatened. We search to hold on to what is most meaningful for us during these late years.

Throughout our lives we make transitions, but I have often claimed that we of the *old* and the *oldest old* are required to make more changes than any other age group. For the most part, we do so with amazing acquiescence. We may not like what is happening, but most of us, without too much protest, make whatever changes are necessary to accommodate our particular circumstances. However, recently I read an article in *The New York Times* ("Think Your Aging Parents Are

Stubborn? Blame 'Mismatched Goals'" September 3, 2019) that reported on some studies of middle-aged children who complained about their aging parents' stubbornness, their persistence in indulging in "insistent" and "risky" behaviors. Some of the stories were indeed surprising. In one, a father refused to follow his doctor's advice regarding biopsies, insisting that he knew what was best. Another who, though severely disabled, would not use a walker since it made him look weak. These complaints of adult children were explained by the researchers as "mismatched goals."

The problem is how to balance safety-versus-autonomy. Children can sometimes over-emphasize safety while parents often place a higher value on autonomy. Such conflicts, if not resolved in a reasonable manner, can lead to avoidance of the contested issues and can disrupt relationships. Social scientists suggest that some older adults find it difficult to receive help. They see it as diminishing their self-perception as always providing help for others—their children, grandchildren, or employees. If these individuals can be offered a way to give support to others, then their self-esteem is improved, and along with it, they experience better health and well-being. All of us want to be needed.

One of the most common areas of conflict centers around driving. For those of us who are old, being able to provide our own transportation gives us freedom of movement and a sense that we are still independent. But there comes a time when our vision, reflexes, and focus become compromised, and we must relinquish that most-valued driver's license. Though I still drive, I have already made considerable modifications. I quit driving at night some time ago, and I no longer drive long distances. (I look back with some nostalgia on those many years when I drove alone from St. Louis to Chicago at least once a month. Also for several years I fearlessly drove the infamous Los Angeles 405 monthly as I headed from LAX up the coast to Santa Barbara.) I like driving and the independence it provides; it will be hard to give it up completely. For now, I am happy that I can drive to my fitness and yoga sessions, can make my way to the grocery store, and to the homes of my friends who live nearby. It is also reassuring to know that cabs and Uber or Lyft are available for those occasions when I do not feel it safe or wise to drive myself.

In addition to the changes in driving, I have let go other activities that I once valued. For example, I no longer entertain at dinner parties the way I once did. Actually I rarely cook, preferring to either eat out or use prepared foods. If friends come for lunch, they bring their own, or we meet in the morning or afternoon without any expectation of being served food. I no longer plant and maintain my garden to the extent I once did, but rely on a small landscape company to do some of that work for me. I seldom go shopping, in part because I do not need more stuff, but also because when it comes to clothing, trying on garments is exhausting! I am careful about walking even moderately long distances. Due to my hearing loss, I no longer go to the theater, attend lectures or workshops; I avoid noisy restaurants, and try to limit the size of the groups I participate in. My life is becoming more constricted.

Sometimes I wonder if I have let go of too much too soon. Am I too accommodating to my perceived failings? Am I too quick to give up when facing difficulties instead of pushing through? One of the researchers pointed out that stubbornness can be a positive trait; it indicates "tenacity, persistence, a sense of control." Do I have enough of those qualities? I wish to be realistic regarding my capabilities, to behave responsibly regarding my health and safety, but I am not a risk-taker. My goal is to remain as active as I can, to keep informed regarding current events, to stay engaged with my friends and family, to continue to exercise and eat a healthy diet. I also believe that indulgence is not always to be avoided; one of my favorite sayings is "Moderation is best in all things, including moderation."

I would like to point out that, though growing old means letting go of many former patterns of behavior, it is essential that we remain open to the ample opportunities for new experiences. Just to mention one, recently I had dinner with a friend at a rooftop restaurant. It was a cool, breezy evening, and I was awed by the joy of sharing good company while looking out over the city, watching the sky turn from light blue to a glorious deep blue as night descended. And then, to top it all off, I rode home in her new red Porsche convertible—with the top down! I never could have imagined having such an exhilarating time at age ninety-one.

Though I have already made quite a few adjustments, I fully realize that there will be more difficult ones to come. Like most people, I would love to remain in my home as long as possible. But I have informed my children that if the time comes when I need special care, then I shall endeavor to accept, perhaps with some reluctance and sorrow, whatever arrangements are necessary.

The danger for us as we grow into very old age is that as we lose control over our outer circumstances, we may also lose sight of who we are and how we view ourselves. It is essential that we retain our sense of self and self-worth so we may continue to feel that our lives have meaning. This means avoiding isolation, paying attention to our thoughts and moods, examining our priorities, and, most importantly, maintaining our relationships with those we love. I hope I can continue to graciously let go of activities and attitudes that no longer serve me well and remain open to dialogue regarding the important matters of safety. I am confident my family will acknowledge my need for as much autonomy as possible given my age and condition, for I know they have my best interests at heart. After all, we are in this together.

AUGUST 2018

Relevance and Irrelevance

Not surprisingly, at my very late stage of life (soon to be ninety), I find that my needs and interests have shifted. Things that once seemed suitable, even highly relevant, now seem unfitting or irrelevant. I want to examine just what those things are and why they hold a different significance, or less prominence, as I have grown old.

For starters, in our culture, where youthfulness is so greatly valued, just being old consigns us to irrelevancy. Having lived past our prime, so it goes, we have little of value to contribute. This pervasive attitude means that we elders are often dismissed and ignored. I heartedly (and heatedly) object to this ageist view and would like to proclaim that we are indeed relevant. Having lived so long, we have much to offer. We know history: it is important to be aware of the past so that we can learn from our mistakes. We old people have experience and skills and insights that can benefit those who follow us. So, irrelevant? No, no, no; we oldsters are decidedly relevant.

But I am aware that some things have indeed grown irrelevant. One of the more obvious and trivial examples is appearance. I still want to be clean, to look nice, to make a good impression. But I do not feel compelled to put forth much effort to accomplish that. Shopping for clothing is a drag. At one time I was careful not to repeatedly wear the same thing. Now I find that it is too much bother to search for a new outfit, so I tend to put on whatever it was I was wearing yesterday. I have several pairs of shoes, but usually just wear my most comfortable ones. If as an old woman I am mostly invisible, does what I wear and how I look really matter? Perhaps just being presentable is enough. Though never high on my list of priorities, fashionable clothing now is certainly irrelevant. Comfort is paramount.

Of greater significance is that the future has become irrelevant. A lot of people enjoy looking at their horoscope daily. They may not really believe in its prognostications, but nevertheless they have an undeniable curiosity regarding its possible bearing on their current and future circumstances. Many of my friends have had their astrological charts drawn and feel they are helpful in indicating which trends their life might follow. Any predictions regarding my life's journey are now completely beside the point. I have, for the most part, already lived my life, have walked my path—for better or worse. Though there may be some unexpected happenings, any predictions about my limited future hold little relevance.

I still have curiosities, but keeping up to date on popular culture no longer seems so important. At one time I had some knowledge of what was playing on Broadway, what books were on the bestseller list, which music groups were most favored. (Of course this was in the days of Joan Baez and Judy Collins.) That is no longer the case. I am less interested in exhibits, lectures, and other cultural events than I once was. Partly this is due to decreased energy, but it is also a shift in the focus of my inquisitiveness. I still try to keep up with national and international news, particularly regarding the current political scene, though at times the information is so upsetting that I must limit my exposure to TV and newspapers. I enjoy reading but do not concentrate on books that are most popular or that convey information. Rather I choose books that examine relationships. Current educational or artistic trends are not without meaning for my stage of life, but admittedly they have less relevance for me now.

This decision to lessen my participation in cultural events suggests a level of withdrawal from former interests and activities and I am aware that too much withdrawal can lead to isolation. I try to remain cognizant of that danger. I continue to strive for a balance between involvement and solitude. I do not wish to participate in endeavors or occasions that fail to nourish me. Just being busy for busyness sake is not beneficial to my mental or physical health. What is relevant is that balance.

Interestingly, time itself has become irrelevant. I do not wear a watch. I feel I have all the time in the world. On the other hand, I know my time is limited. Neither matters. I have few demands and no sense of urgency regarding getting things done. In our early and mid-years, we have many responsibilities—work, family, friends—and never seem to have enough time to attend to our daily tasks. I remember that period of my life, but I no longer have those burdens. I do what I wish to do, which is very little. Now I am content to just *be*, and am not much interested in *doing*. I am pretty much finished with accomplishment. Time holds no power over me.

My priorities around medical care have shifted as well. Some decades ago I quit having routine diagnostic tests—no more mammograms, colonoscopies, blood work, or other medical exams. I have no interest in discovering hidden problems. They will show themselves soon enough and then I will decide what to do. If I do become ill—which is perhaps inevitable at some point—depending on the diagnosis, I may decline treatment if it does not provide ease and comfort. In other words, I am not one to insist on extraordinary measures to stay alive. I will continue to eat well and exercise prudently, both of which are relevant to my health and comfort. I have already lived an incredibly full and meaningful life and have no wish to extend it beyond reasonable expectations.

Which brings up the matter of death. That too has become irrelevant, of little concern. I will die; all of us will die. As I get older, there is no fear, only acceptance, which frees me from anxiety. There is, of course, sadness regarding leaving my loved ones behind. I certainly hope for a peaceful demise, surrounded by my loving family. I know that the end will come; it is part of nature's cycle.

For now, what is most relevant is preserving my relationships with my friends and family. These interactions are what sustain and comfort me. Perhaps the most obvious example of irrelevance is this little essay. What significance do my observations have? Will my comments make any difference in anyone's life? Probably not, but I find pleasure in thinking about these things and sharing them with those I care about. These ruminations help give meaning to my life—and finding meaning is exceedingly relevant.

Lacunae

MARCH 2019

For a few weeks the word *lacuna* (plural *lacunae*) kept coming into my mind. It is not a commonly used word, but for some reason it had special resonance with me as it rang true to some unfortunate experiences I was having. The word refers to a hole, a gap, a lapse, or an absence. Other synonyms, perhaps even more appropriate, are hiatus, break, interruption, void, omission, vacancy, fissure. All relate to what I felt were some weird failures in my usual mental functioning.

Not long ago, a woman in my yoga class came up to me to say that the one thing she most appreciated about my previous book of reflections was my honesty. In these little essays I do try to be as open and honest as I know how, for I want you, my family and friends, to understand as nearly as I can explain just what it is like to grow old. *For me.* I know it is not the same for everyone. I can only relate my own special experiences, though I am sure some of them are more universal to persons of advanced age.

We know that the brain, like other parts of our anatomy, goes through changes as we age. As a result of those physiological changes, we begin to lose words, especially names or proper nouns. Our memory for recent events and thoughts becomes uncertain. Our ability to focus and the capacity to multitask is diminished. Because the brain still has some plasticity, however, we can still learn, create new memories, and improve our language skills. (Perhaps the presence of that odd word *lacuna* is an example of our ability to add to our vocabulary.)

To get to the incidents I experienced that brought about this focus on the *lacunae*, perhaps the most upsetting was locking myself out of my house—on a very cold day! I was able to find a key that I had hidden, but try as I might, I could not get it to work. I knocked on every door in my courtyard, seeking help, but no one was home. I did not have my purse—no money, no phone, no way to call for help. I was freezing and became a bit panicked. I finally decided to go to the next courtyard and fortunately found a family at home. They were extremely gracious, called a locksmith, and offered me a cup of tea while I waited. In the meantime, the husband walked over and was able to unlock the door. I felt a bit foolish as the locksmith had to be canceled, but was extremely grateful for the kindness of the family that offered their help. To me, however, closing the basement door behind me without having my purse was a major lapse. A routine pattern of behavior had truly fallen through a hole in my aging brain. Now I check and double check before I close that door!

Other examples are not quite so extreme, but are nevertheless indicative of some kind of break, or fissure, in my everyday practice—things I usually do without conscious effort or thinking. Not too long ago I had company for dinner. I had prepared the main dish, a salad, a starch, but suddenly realized that I had not remembered to include a green vegetable. Though not of great consequence, still, the omission struck me as unusual. It is not the kind of thing I would have forgotten in the past. What was once habitual, like putting on my hearing aids in the morning, keeping my cell phone with me, and keeping my iPad charged now required more conscious awareness

Another difficulty, though not (yet) extreme, is in determining directions. I do not drive many places that are unfamiliar, but when I do, I find that it takes me a while to sort out just which is the best way to get there. Earlier in my life, that information would have come instantly, but now, it comes slowly. I have to stop and think: Does that street run north and south, or east and west? Can I get there by going this way? So far I have not gotten lost, thank heavens! If I do, I know I can find directions on my phone or, if things get really bad, I can learn to rely on Uber or Lyft.

Recently I lost my credit card. I cannot remember doing that before. I always am extremely careful about putting it back in the same spot in my wallet. I did not realize it was missing until checking out at the grocery store with a very large order. I had to get special approval for my check (which was over one hundred dollars), so it took quite a long time. I felt sorry for all those in the line behind me, waiting patiently for this very flustered old woman who was terrified about her lost card. (Luckily I got a replacement overnight and the old one was never used, so all turned out well.)

Okay! Now that I have exposed the existence of these holes in my brain, I shall also give myself points for recently traveling to Mexico alone. I was immensely touched by the help I received along the way, from airline personnel to incidental persons I met on my journey. By the time I got to Oaxaca, I already knew several people on the plane, anyone of whom would have offered help had I needed it. That experience added to my fundamental belief in the kindness of others. And while I was there my fabulous granddaughters were loving, attentive, and thoughtful in every way. I may have multiple *lacunae*, causing lapses in memory, loss of words, or failure in some routine tasks, but I remain one of the luckiest women alive.

AUGUST 2019

Coping with Hearing Loss

My greatest complaint about being old is my damnable hearing loss. Recently I purchased new hearing aids which have an app that connects calls to my cell phone directly to the hearing aids; intelligibility is much better than on a land line, which frankly is near impossible now. Still, unlike glasses which can usually correct one's vision to almost perfect, hearing aids cannot accomplish that for a hearing loss. Since this is something I must deal with on a daily basis, it occurs to me that it might be helpful for those of you who interact with me to get a little background information about just how this disorder impacts my life. In 1952 I earned a master's degree in Audiology and Speech Pathology, so I understand the limitations of what even the most advanced hearing aids can do and why.

The ear is made up of the exterior part we see, the middle ear which contains a series of small bones that conduct sound vibrations, and the inner ear, which is filled with liquid and contains a spiral with small hair cells that respond to a range of frequencies. When a sound is conveyed to the inner ear, movements of these small hair cells are converted to electrical impulses which are then transmitted to the brain, where the sensation of hearing takes place. What usually happens as we age, is that those hair cells responding to the high frequencies begin to die off at a much faster rate than those responding to lower frequencies. Once the hair cells have died, or their function is impaired, there is no way to replace or repair them. Therefore the frequencies to which they once responded are no longer transmitted; those particular sounds are lost to us.

Our speech is made up of sounds from a wide range of frequencies; vowels are largely in the lower frequency range, whereas many of our consonants, such as *f, t, s, th, sh* are in the high range of normal hearing. With these missing components, speech becomes more and more difficult to understand. That is why many of us who are old can hear some sounds of speech, but cannot understand what is being said. What was once normal conversation becomes difficult, for many words are distorted, becoming unintelligible. Facing the individual who is talking is beneficial, for facial expression and lip movements—lipreading—can be helpful in determining what is being said. But none of that delivers perfect understanding. Having to ask "What?" "Say that again" can be tiresome and frustrating. Pretending to understand what is unclear (which I must admit to doing on occasion) can also lead to embarrassing mistakes or ridiculous misunderstandings.

Another disorder that arises from the aging hearing mechanism is something called *recruitment*. Recruitment increases our sensitivity to loud sounds. Even though there may be only a small increase in the noise level, it feels much louder, causing discomfort. That is why it is so unpleasant for those of us with diminished hearing due to age to be in noisy environments—such as most restaurants. Not only is it more difficult to follow conversation, it can also actually be painful.

I must add to this challenge the fact that my brain, like

that of most old people, processes information much slower than when I was young. When speech is rapid, or mumbled, or when there is an unfamiliar accent with its altered speech patterns, grasping what is said becomes ever more challenging. On the phone I must frequently ask the caller to repeat or to speak more slowly. I have quit going to movies because the dialog is often impossible for me to follow. At home I watch all TV shows with subtitles, which is not a perfect solution, since there is often a long lag, and also quite a bit is omitted, but is certainly better than without them.

This mini-tutorial is provided as a context and explanation for my preference for one-on-one conversations and for quiet environments. I also realize that there are times when larger groups are not only necessary, but welcome. I would not want to give up my family gatherings even though it is impossible for me to take part in exchanges when a large group is around the table, when talk is overlapped, or there is loud laughter, or someone is at the far end of the table. I have learned that during these times, I can no longer be a participant, but must become an observer. It is not always easy, and can be depressing. I want to contribute to the discourse, want to know why people are laughing, but am aware that once the conversation has moved on, or the moment of hilarity is over, there is no recovering it. Accepting this unfortunate fact is one of the many adjustments I am learning to make as I grow old and am losing my hearing.

I am reminded, however, that there are those in between times, when a smaller group—say four or five persons—are involved that presents a different kind of challenge. My inclination is to either act as if I hear or to quietly withdraw from the conversation. Recently I was reminded that it is my responsibility to inform others in small groups if I am not understanding. They can then take appropriate measures to ensure that I am included in the discussion. This is a challenge, and can be awkward, but I realize that it is my obligation to make it known if I am feeling left out. I shall try to remember to do that.

The danger for persons with significant hearing loss, since communication can be so difficult, is to become isolated. So far, I have many friends who come over in the afternoon for one-on-one visits, times that are greatly satisfying. We exchange information, tell stories about our families, share our troubles, or laugh at outlandish things we have heard or done. Restaurants are a greater challenge, for there are few that provide a quiet environment. I have found, however, that if there are only two of us, sitting at the bar is a partial solution, for we are closer together than at a table, can face each other and chat as we drink and eat.

I am writing about hearing loss, which is my particular handicap, but we can glean more general lessons from my experience: we need to be aware of the challenges that others may be facing. Some people have difficulties in mobility, or seeing, or may have momentary confusion, but whatever it is, there exists a shared responsibility. For those of us with the disability, it is helpful to unapologetically make known our needs. For others, it is to be sensitive to and have a willingness to accommodate those special requirements. If we can all remember to do our part, then our interactions with persons with special hardships will be both enjoyable and rewarding.

FEBRUARY 2020

The Loss of Desire

Some weeks ago I became aware that I had descended into a state of lethargy, a dispiritedness that is hard to describe and even harder to fully understand. As I began to ponder just what was going on and why, it occurred to me that what I was experiencing was a *loss of desire*. Could this possibly be a sign of mild depression? In many respects it feels normal; after all I am in my nineties, a time of natural decline. (Though I am reminded of a book called *Declining to Decline*.) I cannot help but wonder if this loss is appropriate, if it might have some advantages, or if it is an undesirable change in my outlook.

As I see it, desire is a yearning for something or someone that presumably would, by its (or his/her) presence, supplant a sense of absence or emptiness. My dictionary says it is "an unsatisfied longing or craving." Psychologists view desire as arising from the body, such as a desire for food. In my case the diminishing desire I feel is for certain kinds of activities. For example, I do not wish for more stuff, so shopping brings no pleasure. Visiting museums is tiring and no longer brings inspiration. Hearing loss has created frustration as the dialogue in lectures, movies, or plays is often unintelligible, so attending them is frustrating. Travel is exhausting and therefore not appealing. Dining out remains enjoyable, but the usual noisy environments make conversation difficult, so even this is less desirable than it once was.

In my earlier life I was filled with desires—for beautiful things, security, knowledge and understanding, new experiences, travel, and most especially, for greater love. There seemed not to be enough to satisfy my yearnings. It was these obsessive desires I felt as a young woman that drove me to run away from home to be with the man I loved, have a family, pursue an education, embrace my many interests, work with disabled children, travel, delight in homemaking, make friends, and follow my creative urges in sewing, music, photography, rituals, and writing. Desire provides motivation, gets us moving both physically and mentally, and fulfills our ambitions, enriches our lives, and provides us with the impetus to deepen our knowledge and broaden our perspectives. It offers us an opportunity to develop wisdom.

It is important to acknowledge that as constructive as desire can be, it can also be a detriment. If we are too intensely invested in the outcome of our yearnings, they can become overpowering. As the Buddhists point out, too much attachment to the object of our desire can cause suffering. I have often experienced such suffering myself. I have been crushed when my carefully made plans did not unfold as I had hoped, hurt when the respect or love I longed for did not meet my expectations or perceived needs, disheartened when I failed to live up to my own high standards of behavior. Overwhelming desire for something unobtainable or unavailable or unwise can cause enormous anguish. I have reaped the benefits of desire but also have known the frustration and sorrow resulting from deep attachments to desires unmet.

I am reminded of three important attributes as we grow old: patience, acceptance, and detachment, qualities that have special relevance to this discussion. I can avoid some suffering and enjoy a more peaceful old age as I become more patient with my own limitations and those of others, as I develop more acceptance of whatever path lies before me or whatever shortcomings I may have, and as I am able to establish some emotional detachment from the wished-for outcome of the desires I have left.

In some ways, the loss of desire is liberating and fosters a feeling of contentment. I am freed from focusing on what is missing; many of those former desires are either fulfilled or are no longer relevant. For now, my needs are simple. I find myself more and more satisfied with my constricted life style. I am happy to remain at home, to read, to keep up with political affairs or watch the occasional movie on TV. I enjoy simple meals, going early to bed, sleeping as late as I wish, visiting with friends, or writing an occasional reflection.

Can contentment sometimes bleed over into apathy? Can too much satisfaction foster a withdrawal from the joys and trials of life? Perhaps. I must remain aware of the dangers of being too removed from the connections and relationships that give me sustenance. If desire is absent, what propels me forward? Perhaps that word *forward* is a clue, because what I truly desire is to delve deeper into my inner life, to go inward. (These reflections are a consequence of that aspiration.) So, perhaps it is natural for me to recede into relative solitude in order to reserve my limited energy. I want to spend my free time contemplating how best to continue finding meaning during my remaining years and participating in the things that I continue to truly desire.

Foremost among those is a need for meaningful relationships. Spending time and exchanging views with members of my family and with my friends are my highest priorities. Those occasions when family members come for a few days or when friends come over for an afternoon visit give me the greatest pleasure. I also find great enjoyment in the small discussion groups to which I belong. I look forward to those occasions, and would feel bereft if they were no longer available.

I recently found this quote from the *Tao Te Ching*:

Free from desire, you realize the mystery.
Caught in desire, you see only the manifestations.
Yet mystery and manifestations
arise from the same source.
The source is called darkness.
Darkness within darkness
The gateway to all understanding.

Free from desire, you realize the mystery. My effort at understanding my loss of desire perhaps only plunges me into darkness, that mysterious inner realm wherein lies *the gateway to all understanding.*

DECEMBER 2019

Becoming a Sage

In my large file of poems, I recently found one titled "Becoming the Possible Sage." I have no idea how I came to possess it. No author's name is attached, but there is this notation: "With help from *The Sage's Tao Te Ching*, by William Martin." I ordered Martin's book in which he describes the Tao as a practical guide to a way of life involving awareness, simplicity, and contentment, an approach that resonates with my own. The poem by the unknown author is a collection of some of the passages from Martin's book. This discovery led to a fascinating series of synchronicities. But first, here is the poem:

If you are becoming a sage
you will grow in trust and contentment.
You will discover the light
of life's deepest truths.
If you are merely growing older,
you will become trapped by fears and frustrations.
You will see only the darkness
of infirmity and death.
There is one primary choice
facing every aging person:
Will we become sages
harvesting the spiritual essence of our lives
and blessing future generations?
Or will we just grow older,

circling the wagons,
and waiting for the end?
Being a sage is not all unruffled calm.
It is also a time of freedom
to express and feel
the truth of our lives.
To explore the passions
buried for years
beneath acceptable masks.
It is time to serve a cause
with energy and compassion,
to fall madly in love
and dance into the night.
Don't accept the modern myths of aging.
You are not declining.
You are not fading away into uselessness.
You are a sage,
a river at its deepest
and most nourishing.
Do not succumb to the lie
that the second half of life
should be a time of increasing luxury and ease.
Baubles galore are offered to older persons
as seeming rewards for all their work.
The sage sees these trinkets as symbols
of foolishness, not of power.
The sage sees life in deeper ways,
sees intricate patterns of beauty
embedded in life's fabric,

sees comfort woven within the pain,
sees gain shining amidst the loss;
sees forgiveness binding up resentment's wounds;
and sees life always rising out of death.
Healing of this world's painful wounds
is now your task,
and the healing of your own is the first step.
It is time to lay aside the ambition
that has perpetuated wounding,
and let your growing contentment
speak of another way.
You can train your mind
through meditation, reading,
and mental exercise.
You can train your body through yoga, T'ai Chi,
and physical exercise.
You can train your heart
through listening, accepting,
and forgiving all.
Having nothing more to gain,
nothing left to finish,
leaves us calm
and able to see without fear.
Therefore we bring clarity to confusion,
and comfort to suffering.

Some of the strangely connected events regarding this poem took place many years ago, others more recently. My recollections and my more recent experiences have aroused a sense of wonder and a curiosity about the concept of synchronicity as outlined by Carl Jung. The first incident happened about twenty years ago when I had a dream that I still remember vividly. In the dream I am seated in a large, leather-covered, overstuffed chair in a room with a decided Chinese décor. I am alone, fascinated by my unusual surroundings. For some reason I reach down between the cushion and the chair and discover a small book; it is a copy of *The Tao Te Ching*.

This was a curious dream because, though I had heard of the book, I was not very familiar with it. A few days later I received an invitation to attend a weekend workshop in Ojai, California, on T'ai Chi and the Tao. I was immediately struck by the coincidence and felt I must attend. (Ojai is not far from Santa Barbara, where I was a student at Pacifica Graduate Institute.) The man leading us in the movements of T'ai Chi was also a calligrapher. As he lectured on the Tao, he illustrated many of its concepts. There was an exhibit of his work at a local gallery, so after the workshop ended I went with a friend. Before I had seen any of the other work, a calligraph immediately caught my eye. I told my friend: "I want that one." When I walked over to take a closer look, I was astonished to find that the title was "The Tao." Another strange coincidence! I purchased it, had it framed, and it has hung in my living room ever since.

Occasionally I have quoted a line or two from an old copy I have of *The Tao Te Ching*, but I cannot say that I had thought about it very much until I discovered Martin's book on the sage. *The Tao Te Ching* is often translated as "the way of life." The central character is described as a person whose life is in perfect harmony with the way things are. Recently I looked again at the introduction to Martin's book and discovered that it was written by Chungliang Al Huang. He is the man who had conducted the workshop and the artist of the work that hangs in my living room. Another interesting coincidence.

A few days ago I was upstairs looking for another book when my hand fell on one by Jean Shinoda Bolen, a Jungian analyst, titled *The Tao of Psychology: Synchronicity and the Self*, published in 1982. Well! I could no longer believe these were just random occurrences. Its unexpected appearance following all the other instances involving the Tao surely indicates that something is at work here. Jung described synchronicity as an acausal connecting principle that manifests itself through meaningful coincidences. The link between these coincidences cannot be explained by cause and effect or grasped intellectually, rather it requires an intuitive quality. It is the subjective experience of awe and wonder at the connectivity of seemingly random occurrences that creates synchronicity.

Bolen likens synchronistic events to dreams. As she writes, "Synchronicity is like a waking dream in which we experience the point of intersection of the timeless with time, where the impossible union of spheres of existence is actual, and where what is inside of us and what is outside of us is unseparated. Like a dream, synchronicity reveals something we dimly grasp, glimpses of the underlying Tao." She further points out that one of the lessons synchronicity teaches us is a *greater comprehension of the underlying oneness of all things, a sense that we are a small part of a greater whole.* There are some parallels among the psychological, the mystical, the paranormal, and even quantum theory in which the observer cannot be separated from that which is observed, for each of these points to the interconnectedness of all phenomena.

Bolen relates a famous story about a rainmaker that illustrates the relationship between synchronicity and the Tao. In the story a country was suffering from a prolonged drought when an old man appeared who asked only for a quiet little house where he locked himself inside for three days. On the fourth day it began to rain. The man said that he was not responsible for the rain but that he had come from another country where all was in order. When he arrived at this place he found things were not as they should be, that the whole country was not in Tao, was in fact disordered, a circumstance that affected him as well. Therefore he had to wait three days until he was back in Tao and then naturally the rain came.

Bolen points out that psychologically the story of the rainmaker suggests that to be back in Tao is to experience being part of "the oneness that underlies and nourishes all things, to connect again with what Jung calls the Self, to feel the abundance of love which is available both to give and to receive." It is to feel centered again and to be in touch with a sense that life has meaning. Regarding the rainmaker, it also tells us that "If the inner world is reflected in the outer world through synchronicity, then returning to the Tao inwardly of course resulted in a return of the rain, as a restoration of the natural order."

As I took a break from writing this commentary on the rainmaker story, I decided to watch a movie on my TV. The first movie shown in a list of possibilities was, believe it or not, "The Rainmaker." Of course I watched it. The following night, again after working on this reflection, I picked up a volume of poetry called *ten poems to last a lifetime*, works selected by Roger Housden. I opened it at random and quite astonishingly this is the poem I found on that page: "The Mind of Absolute Trust" by Seng-Ts'an, translated by Stephen Mitchell. The poem, of course, is about the Tao. The opening lines are

The Great Way isn't difficult
for those who are unattached to their preferences.
Let go of longing and aversion
and everything will be perfectly clear.

The second section of the poem begins

If you don't live in the Tao,
you fall into assertion or denial.
Asserting that the world is real,
you are blind to its deeper reality;
denying that the world is real,
you are blind to the selflessness of all things.
The more you think about these matters,
the farther you are from the truth.

Synchronistic experiences usually connote something psychologically important though it may not be immediately understood. This sequence of events surely seems to have some meaning, as if a message is being delivered to me. So I now must pause and reflect in order to fully comprehend the significance of the Tao in my life. Perhaps I can find more harmony. I also might add my hope that we soon find a rainmaker who can bring more order to our disordered country.

DEATH

JUNE 2020

The Squirrel

Each morning before I prepare my breakfast, I walk outside into my garden, greeting the new day and silently expressing my gratitude for the plants and flowers that give so generously of their beauty. This morning I noticed a young squirrel in a fetal position lying on the walk. He did not scamper away when I entered the garden as most squirrels do. I thought perhaps he was injured. I didn't know what to do, so I turned to my trusted source, Google, asking, "What do I do with an injured squirrel?"

It instructed me to cover the animal with a towel and place it in a box, and then contact an agency that deals with caring for injured wild animals. After I finished my breakfast I got a box from the basement, took a towel and slowly approached the squirrel. To my surprise and relief, he scurried into some plants nearby. So I decided to get on with my day and headed out to my fitness session. When I returned more than an hour later, the squirrel was back on the walk sprawled out on all fours, and looked very sick. When I approached this time, he did not move. I could see that he was still breathing, his sides expanding and contracting with each breath. I had the sense that he was dying and my intuition was that I should leave him to die an easy and peaceful death. Sometime later I checked on him again and determined that indeed he was no longer breathing.

Since I have many squirrels that forage and root through my garden, I assume that this young one must be an offspring of one of my regular visitors. It seemed only appropriate that he be buried in my garden. I got a shovel, dug a hole in a rather secluded spot, and placed him in the grave. Hoping that he "Rest in Peace," I said a few words of blessing and covered him with dirt.

This incident strikes me as very strange. I have never heard of a sick wild animal choosing to come to an enclosed garden for his last hours of life. It was odd that though he had found enough strength to hide himself among the plants when I initially approached him, once I was gone, he obviously crept back onto the sidewalk to die in full view. Why didn't he remain in the shrubbery? Did he choose a spot where he knew he would be seen? That seems very un-squirrel-like.

What am I to make of this? Is there a message to be found in this unusual occurrence? I do not know, but I do know that I am deeply touched. Death comes to all of us, and I am grateful that this little animal's remains will always be a part of my beautiful garden.

NOVEMBER 2020

The Hawk

As I walked to the sliding glass doors to look out on my garden, I was startled to see a hawk perched on the patio table. He looked anxious, jerking his head back and forth, as if fearing he might be seen. I was even more startled when I realized that underneath his claws was a small, bloodied chipmunk that he was about to devour. I have often seen a chipmunk scurrying about in my garden, so perhaps the hawk had spied him there, though I did not witness the hunt. A part of me was horrified, but I immediately realized that I could hardly blame the hawk for following his nature, after all, I also eat meat.

Moving as carefully and quietly as I could, I came back occasionally to watch. Having decided that he was in a secure place to finish his meal, he stayed at least an hour. When he had flown away, I went outside and was astonished to see that all that was left on the table were a few tiny bones. Miraculously, the hawk had consumed every bit of flesh and fur of the little animal. He must have been a very hungry hawk.

I think of my garden as a sanctuary, a safe and secure place. It is that, but it is also part of the natural world. Birds sip water as they land on the flat rock where water flows continuously from the motor in my little pond. Squirrels forage for their hidden treasures. Butterflies flit about. Bees feast on the nectar of the flowers. Unseen insects dine on foliage. Life abounds, as does death. The same week the hawk visited, I found the remains of a bird, only its feathers and feet, the rest having been eaten.

If there is a lesson to be found in seeing the beautiful hawk gorge himself on the innocent chipmunk and finding the residue of the bird, it is a reminder that we humans are also animals, predators, sharing this chain of life and death. I search for insight, for some deeper meaning to be gained from these extraordinary, yet ordinary happenings, but mostly I am in awe. Seeing the hawk live out his hawk-essence was an awe-full sight, one I shall never forget. The memory and the mystery add to the depth and richness of what my garden means to me.

Regrets

MAY 2019

Recently I came across a post from a nurse who described what she had observed as the "top five regrets people make on their deathbed." I have often thought about the concept of regret, and this report prompted me to delve a bit more deeply into this topic which has particular relevance for this stage of my life. I believe there are worthwhile lessons here for all of us, regardless of age.

The most common is this: *I wish I'd had the courage to live a life true to myself, not the life others expected of me.* I was surprised that in the nurse's experience this was the most common regret, but I agree that not to have lived an authentic life would certainly be an enormous loss. It seems that people when their lives are almost over suddenly have to acknowledge that their lack of fulfillment was due to choices they had made, or not made. They are aware that many of their dreams have gone unfulfilled, perhaps because of an inability to counter cultural or familial expectations. As the nurse says, "It is very important to try and honour at least some of your dreams along the way. From the moment that you lose your health, it is too late. Health brings a freedom very few realise until they no longer have it."

This is one regret I do not have. Once I decided to run away from my home in North Carolina at age eighteen, and perhaps even earlier, I knew I was not destined to live the life my parents expected of me. I am not sure how I came to that fundamental understanding, but after my first year at Washington University in St. Louis, my father declared that if I chose not to go along with his way of life, then he would not support me in college. (Along with other issues, such as his Southern Baptist religious beliefs, which I rejected, he insisted that I accept racial segregation as okay.) At that moment I knew it was time for me to break away from that constricted life and follow my own path. I have never regretted that decision; in fact I remain in awe of my eighteen-year-old self who saw so clearly that she had to be true to herself.

Largely I have remained faithful to this effort. In fact, I see the primary aim of my Jungian analysis (which I entered in my sixties) as a desire to understand more deeply and to establish more firmly my authentic selfhood. Among other endeavors, becoming a photographer, going back to school in my late years, and writing books, were ways of living into and validating who I am as a person, beyond what my parents could have allowed, or even imagined. I can now identify myself not only as a wife, mother, grandmother, and great-grandmother, but also as a woman with her own distinctive talents, skills, and intellectual abilities.

The second most frequent regret was: *I wish I didn't work so hard.* The nurse said that this comment came from every male patient she attended. They regretted spending so much of their lives at work, not having enough time with their young children or their partners. Her suggestion is to simplify our lifestyles and acknowledge that we do not need the income we think we do. Furthermore, if we create more space in our lives, we "become happier and more open to new opportunities."

I was largely a stay-at-home Mom, only working part time after my girls were in school, so this regret does not specifically apply to me. I will say, however, that though my husband was an entrepreneur and was devoted to the success of his company, he came home for dinner every night. If additional work needed to be done, he brought it home on the weekends. Time for his family was an important priority. I shall always be grateful for that.

The third most common regret was: *I wish I'd had the courage to express my feelings.* The nurse says that many of us suppress our feelings in order to keep peace with others. As a result, she writes, we settle for a mediocre existence and never become who we are truly capable of becoming. She suggests that the resulting bitterness and resentment can lead to illness. A remedy is the realization that we cannot control the reactions of others. So, if we decide to speak honestly, "in the end it brings the relationship to a whole new and healthier level." Of course, as she acknowledges, it can also end a relationship, but perhaps, she suggests, it was too unhealthy to be continued. "Either way, you win."

This is a challenging one for me. Though I certainly agree that expressing our true feelings can often enhance and deepen our relationships, there are some occasions when it is better to keep quiet, "to keep peace," to acknowledge calmly to oneself that our true feelings are too threatening or too potentially explosive to share with those we love. There were many times when I did not dare speak my truth, for I knew it would endanger my marriage, and I did not want to risk that. For example, there was a time in my marriage when I felt strongly that Norm needed to see a therapist. I urged him to do so, but one day he told me that if I ever mentioned it again, he would leave. Though I still think I was correct—that both he and our relationship would have benefitted from more psychological insight, I did not bring it up again. In this case, suppressing my feelings was necessary in order to save my marriage, and I do not regret having made that decision.

The fourth regret mentioned is: *I wish I had stayed in touch with my friends.* Sometimes those in the final weeks of their lives realize that they have lost touch with old friends, but it is now too late to recover that connection. Friendships require time and attention and all too often people get caught up in their everyday responsibilities. They forget to make time to attend to relationships. When we are near death our friends become ever more precious to us.

Though I am not near death (so far as I know), I truly value my friends and make every effort to stay in touch. My awareness of the importance of friends has deepened as I have grown older, and I am mindful of how much their love and friendship mean to me. If it becomes clear that my death is impending, I hope to have my friends come, hold my hands, talk to me, perhaps sing to me. As the nurse says, love and relationships are all that remain in the final weeks of life.

The final regret listed was: *I wish I had let myself be happier.* This suggests that happiness is a choice and that all too often we remain stuck in old, familiar, damaging patterns of thought and behavior. The nurse observes, "Fear of change had them pretending to others, and to their selves, that they were content. When deep within, they longed to laugh properly and have silliness in their life again." She says that when we are on our deathbed, we no longer are concerned about what people think of us, so long before we are dying, we should "let go and smile again." As she recommends, "Life is a choice. It is YOUR life. Choose consciously, choose wisely, choose honestly. Choose happiness."

Again, I do not feel this one applies to me, at least not at this stage of my life. I am not certain one can "choose happiness." I suffered from depression when I was younger. I wish I had not been depressed, but I do not think it was something I chose. I would have preferred not to be miserable and worked hard at overcoming my despondency. As I have grown older I have become more centered and more content. Contentment is my preferred state of being. I view happiness as emerging spontaneously when special occasions elicit it. I think of myself as possibly a bit serious, but not somber; I smile and laugh with my friends and family.

As so often happens when I begin considering a topic, something comes to my attention that has some bearing on what I am writing about. Today (May 18, 2019) there is an op-ed in *The New York Times* by Roger Cohen titled "Reflections on the Graduation of My Daughter." He writes of tears flowing as the youngest of his four children graduates college and then admits that in addition to the tears there was remorse. "I could have been a better dad, more present, more patient, more understanding, less consumed by the next deadline…. [I]t's the amount of love a child receives that builds the surest foundation for happiness. Not for success, however that is measured, but for happiness."

Just as Cohen acknowledges his shortcomings as a father, I know I have hurt people that I love, and have been hurt by some of them, but I prefer not to dwell on the hurt, but rather to focus on the healing that takes place when we reach a deeper understanding of our individual differences and perspectives. Though I have made many mistakes, and often acted out of ignorance or misunderstanding, I like to believe that I did the best I could given the circumstances I faced.

Cohen points out that he could have done worse, but does not see that as an excuse. "There's no point in taking stock unless it's unsparing; and there's no other way to change." He goes on to say that "Life is a riddle whose only imperfect solution is love. Love cheats time because it's passed along, refracted through the generations and it's the reason, with all its illusions, that we're here in the first place." His words deeply touch the essence of what it is I wish to hand on to my family.

When I look back on the nine decades of my life, I primarily feel astonishment. I am in awe of all that I have seen and done. It is difficult to fathom how I have come so far. Was I really once a little Southern farm girl, feeling unloved, sad, and lonely? I made my own way as a young woman by leaving behind family and many Southern ways. As an undergraduate, I married an atheistic Jew and insisted that I continue my education alongside him. After we received our Master's degrees, I was fortunate to find work as an audiologist, and later to have explored creative activities such as photography. I was open to continued learning, and eventually, at age 73, got a PhD. I am proud to have written four books. I am constantly astounded to find myself the matriarch of an extraordinary family—all of whom are attentive, responsible, intelligent, kind, and loving. I have been blessed beyond any dreams I might have had. I have had a truly fulfilled, good life. Like most of us, I certainly had troubles and challenges, but largely I overcame them. I am forever amazed at and grateful for the rich life I have led. So, *no regrets!*

OCTOBER 2019
A Funeral and Lessons Learned

Sara died last week. She was 99 years old. A remarkable woman. She was my husband's first cousin and best friends with Norm's sister Jeanette who, in her fifties, died of ovarian cancer in 1976. I entered this Jewish family in 1948, still an undergraduate, barely 20, a young "shiksa" and decided outsider. All members of Norm's family were kind to me, accepted me lovingly, without judgment regarding my Southern Baptist upbringing, for which I remain forever grateful.

I was especially drawn to these two women, Sara and Jeanette, who were about a decade older than I, already with established families. But I was more than a little intimidated by the special bond they had from growing up together. They had shared many common experiences and had developed a deep friendship. I wanted their approval and their guidance, wanted to be a part of their exceptional connection, but was not sure how to get it.

Jeanette's early death was a tragedy for her immediate family, and also a huge loss for the rest of us. In many ways she had been the glue that held the extended family together. I wondered what my relationship with Sara would be; acutely aware that I could not in any way take Jeanette's place, but hoped that we would become closer. I need not have worried, for Sara, in her open-hearted and genial way, embraced me fully. Over the years I got to know and appreciate her unique personality.

The word that first comes to my mind when I think of Sara is *gracious*, at all times tactful and cordial. She displayed genuine interest in what was going on in my life and that of my family. She greeted me each time I saw her with, "How are you? And how are the kids?" Sara had a wry sense of humor; she could see the absurdities of life. I remember a period during our get-togethers when she'd share a new joke, more often than not it was a bit racy. She also was an astute observer, not one to suffer fools gladly and never hesitant to express her opinions.

Sara also was an avid reader, especially of the daily paper, and kept abreast of political issues which contributed to our lively conversations. There was no doubt about her liberal orientation, going back as far as her work on behalf of Adlai Stevenson, presidential candidate in 1952 and 1956, when he was the Democratic nominee. Both times he was defeated, but her dedication to democratic values never wavered. She was appalled by President Trump.

Neither of Sara's children had children, which undoubtedly was a loss for her. She never complained about that, but did sometimes express her concern about who would take care of her children when they grew old. She often spoke of how fortunate she was that they were always loving and attentive to her. I was impressed and touched that she never in any way made me (or anyone else) feel that we needed to lessen our pride regarding our own grandchildren. It was another measure of her extraordinary graciousness.

In her late years Sara had many challenges. She was hard of hearing, developed lymphoma, fell and broke her pelvis. In her last year she broke her hip and moved three times to various residential care centers. On more than one occasion it seemed that she might be close to the end of her long life. After one of these recent episodes she slept for about three days. Everyone thought this was surely it—but on the third day, she woke up, said, "Well, that didn't work! I guess I'm not dying." Then she got out of bed and went to lunch. She was ready to let go, but her body was not quite ready to give up. Until it did. Then she went peacefully, ready for the passage out of this world into the mysterious beyond. So, I was not sad, for I knew she welcomed death. As the (female) Rabbi said, "Birth is the beginning, and death is the destination." Sara had reached her destination.

Sara's funeral was a loving tribute to her and held some lessons for me. She was not a religious person, but she most certainly identified strongly with her Jewish culture and background. The Rabbi talked briefly, but it was the eulogies delivered by her children and a young cousin that made up the essence of the graveside service. I could not help but think that now I am the only survivor of that generation. Most likely, it is I who will be next to bring our extended family together for a funeral or memorial service. It was impossible for me to avoid thinking about what it might be like when I am the one who has decided to let go of this life.

As the casket was lowered by mechanical means into the earth at a gravesite next to her husband's, another thought occurred to me. I was happy that I had arranged for a green burial, without embalming, and without a casket. My body will be wrapped in a simple white linen shroud and lowered into a shallow grave by means of fabric loops. In the Reform Jewish funerals I have attended (including Sara's), after the prayers and eulogies are finished and the casket is lowered, attendees each shovel dirt on top of the casket. I am told that this tradition symbolizes placing a warm blanket over a loved one. In any case, it is a lovely custom. When I am laid to rest I hope earth and flowers will be strewn on my gravesite.

But perhaps the most important lesson I learned at Sara's memorable and moving funeral was that what really matters are the memories that those who knew and loved us consider most important and meaningful. The tributes to Sara were filled with funny, loving anecdotes that illustrated the respect and love that she shared with her family and friends. I have on my desktop computer a file titled "Death Info, Leah." It is filled with information that I have imagined my family might want to know regarding how I wish to be treated as I near the end of life. It also has some suggestions for a possible funeral or memorial service. After attending Sara's funeral I realize how superfluous and meaningless much of that information is. It really does not matter which poems or songs or readings are presented when the time comes for my service. My preferences or tastes are really not relevant for that occasion. My time will have passed. I understand now that if my loved ones speak from their hearts with the kind of humor and genuine love that I heard from Sara's loved ones, then I will be more than fulfilled.

JULY 2020

Do I Matter?

A counselor who specializes in end-of-life concerns recently told a friend that an important need as we face death is to feel that we matter. When she shared this comment, my immediate response was haughty dismissal: "That is just not true! I do not matter, and I do not care in the least whether or not I matter." The question of whether or not I mattered had never consciously occurred to me, but her suggestion motivated me to examine the meaning of the word more closely and to scrutinize the reasons for my impulsive reaction.

The verb form of the word *matter* means "to be of importance, to have significance." I have never thought of myself as a person of importance, and certainly in the broad scheme of things I am not. Nor have I ever aspired to be seen as having any particular significance. I once wrote a reflection defending the concept of mediocrity; I continue to be fully satisfied with my mediocre accomplishments. It was within that context that the matter of mattering aroused my initial response. However, as I have thought about this question of what desires or needs might feel important when I am near death, perhaps it is worthwhile to acknowledge these.

Our personal, psychological structure has roots in our family of origin and in our most enduring relationships. These intimate associations—parents, siblings, husbands, wives, partners, friends—are foundational in determining whether our fundamental emotional needs are met or are denied. I have long realized that one of my emotional trigger points is whether or not I feel respected. I did not get the kind of intellectual respect through much of my life that I desired and deserved. But having lived long enough to demonstrate my sufficient intellectual capabilities by earning a PhD late in life, and by possessing friendships with those whose intellects I greatly admire, I no longer feel a lack of respect.

Another persistent wish has been that my family remain close. I am sure this grows out of the fact that I missed that kind of family unity in my own growing up. Even as a child, though I had cousins living nearby, I did not feel close to any of them. And then, having basically severed relationships with my parents at age eighteen, I lost any opportunity of ever knowing what it might be like to be a part of a loving, cohesive clan. So now that I have my own family, it is of great importance to me that my children, grandchildren, and great-grandchildren experience the joy of being together at extended family gatherings. The difficulty of arranging that in this time of pandemic is one of my greatest sorrows.

There is one other need that I must acknowledge, and that is that my family understand my basic values. It is not that they are unaware of these; surely they are. But many years ago I felt a need to put it all in writing. I suppose one can call this a concern regarding my legacy. I wrote ten typed pages titled "An Ethical Will." Unlike a legal will that deals with the distribution of material goods, an ethical will focuses on the nonmaterial facets of our lives. My ethical will offers a little personal history as well as some of the thoughts, feelings, and values that I find important and wish to share with those who follow me. The topics I address are Family, Relationships, Education, Creativity, Social Responsibility and Politics, Spiritual Pursuits and Inner Work, Forgiveness, and a Conclusion that lists some suggestions that I have found useful in my life. I placed this nonlegal will in the file on my computer titled "Death Info, Leah," perhaps to be read at the time of my death.

It occurs to me that I would not have been moved to write this ethical will had I not felt, and admittedly continue to feel, that who I am and what I believe has some value—that I matter—and that my comments might have some positive influence on my children, grandchildren, and great-grandchildren. Contrary to my initial response of "I don't care if I matter!", the fact is, how I am perceived by my family is of immense importance to me. I read this document every few months, and make edits if needed to more accurately represent my current way of thinking. I confess that I wish to convey those attitudes and goals that I feel are both important and laudable, worthy of emulation, and that my words will be remembered as a kind of legacy.

Recently I received this definition of legacy from an organization that trains end of life doulas. I do not know who wrote it, but I was struck right away with the thought that having an impact on others certainly implies that we have mattered.

Legacy is the impact a person has had—conscious or unconscious—on the people and world around them. Simply by living, a person has impact. In being a part of a family, raising children, participating in a circle of friends, going to work, taking a role in the community, in every sphere of life, a person leaves their imprint, just as walking across wet cement will leave footprints that solidify and remain. Most of the time, a person moves through the events of their life without thinking much about their legacy, in the same way that they probably didn't consider meaning. But in the doula approach to end of life, meaning and legacy are two of the most important elements preceding the time a person will start actively dying.

When I am nearing death I do not anticipate being troubled about whether I mattered, for in my heart I know that I am respected, am confident that my family will remain devoted, and that my legacy will be honored. I also know that I am loved. What more can one ask?

MAY 2019

Harvesting

There is a poem on my desk written by John O'Donohue titled "For Old Age." It opens with these lines: "May I be given wisdom for the eyes of my soul / To see this as a time of precious harvesting." Those lines prompted me to ponder the idea of *harvest* and *harvesting*. In one way, spring seems a strange topic for this time of year; we usually think of harvest as related to fall when grains and other crops are gathered. Right now I am enjoying a magnificent spring, my garden lush with new growth and bursting with color. But seen as a late stage of life, as O'Donohue's title suggests, it now seems an appropriate time for me to contemplate just what *harvesting* signifies.

I remembered that 25 years ago, in 1994, Harvest was the theme for our annual Thanksgiving ritual. I found a copy of the letter I sent to the family and the outline of the ritual. Sadly there is no record of what each of us said. (How I wish I had that!) However, the questions I posed then remain relevant for me now, and actually for all of us, no matter our age or the season.

The first question was "What does it mean 'to harvest'?" Synonyms are "yield, gather, collect, garner, ingather, bring in." In psychological terms, perhaps "to harvest" suggests bringing into our conscious awareness the fruits of our everyday lives, the effects of our existence. We can benefit enormously from thinking about just what or how our actions contribute to the betterment of our personal lives and of society. We can also focus on what we have gathered from others, a personal collection, a harvest of information and understanding.

The second question was "When does harvest take place? Is it limited to a particular season?" Though as I mentioned, we may immediately think of autumn, there are many fruits and berries that ripen early in the springtime. This is analogous to the attitudes and actions that mature in the early years of our lives. In our youth we study, learn, work, adjust to difficult and changing situations, engage in intimate relationships, perhaps celebrate the arrival of children. As we grow older, we gather other experiences: moving, promotions, failures, illness, recovery, divorce, dissolution of old and establishment of new friendships, even the deaths of those we love. As long as we strive to remain aware, these experiences are also a kind of harvesting, an ingathering of acceptance and wisdom that is not limited to any particular age or season. So actually we are harvesting throughout the span of our lives.

Third was "What can we do to insure a bountiful harvest in our lives?" Again, I think this refers to our ability to pay close attention to the consequences of our behavior. If we live with integrity, authenticity, and try to be as honest and open as we know how to be, then our harvest will indeed be plentiful. Our thoughts and behaviors will sow seeds in all of those who know and love us and will multiply beyond the scope of our imagination. We are not always aware of how important even our most casual and incidental encounters may be, so it behooves us to try to always remember to be considerate, even to those whose response may be indifferent or hostile.

My final item was not a question, but a suggestion: "Thank someone at the table for their contribution to your personal harvest." This is a recommendation that has taken on greater significance as I have grown older. I realize now that when I was young, my own insecurities and vulnerabilities made it difficult for me to admit how much I valued and appreciated the knowledge, expertise, beauty, and wisdom that family, friends, and acquaintances offered to me. I hope I have become better at acknowledging those gifts as I have grown old.

So, when O'Donohue talks about old age as "a time of precious harvesting," I think he means that it is a stage of life when we more deeply realize and can more openly express our gratitude for all that we have gathered from those around us. I know I would not be the person I am today had it not been for the love and support of my family and friends. All in all it has been a very good life. I have been blessed with a bountiful harvest.

O'Donohue's final verses offer a valuable benediction for each of us:

May I have a great dignity,
And a sense of how free I am,
Above all, may I be given the wonderful gift
Of meeting the eternal light that is within me.

May I be blessed;
And may I find a wonderful Love
in myself for myself.

JULY 2019

A Good Death

I have had a very good life. Now what I wish for is a good death. How can that be accomplished? My granddaughter Jessie recently sent me an article about end of life doulas. I had never heard of such a thing. Most of us are aware of birthing doulas, usually women, who provide guidance and support to pregnant women during delivery. They often remain to offer additional support during the postpartum period. We all know that giving birth is a profound experience, and having someone in attendance who has sensitivity, knowledge, and sympathetic understanding can be enormously helpful. Death is an equally profound passage, and it makes sense that having an experienced person to assist in that transition can also be comforting. End of life doulas provide comfort not only to the dying person, but also to the family and loved ones who are witnessing the inevitable and mysterious transition from life to death.

When I first heard about this, I thought about becoming an end of life doula. The International End of Life Doula Association (INELDA) is an organization that offers weekend workshops around the United States and grants certification upon course completion. But the training seemed quite intense, requiring long days of participation, and I was not sure I had the stamina for that. I also harbored some doubt about marketing myself as a certified professional death doula. Perhaps it is because I have always appreciated the value of ritual that I am so enamored by the thought of marking the passage from life to death with a celebration, granting the dying an opportunity to pass on with as much conscious awareness as possible. My idea of an end of life doula would be someone who could help me live life as fully as I can up to the very end.

When I think more about this concept, I realize that as a family we already know how to do this. We have participated in rituals for decades and I am confident the thought of ritualizing the dying process does not seem alien. Though we did not have a formal ritual at the time, I have always thought that my husband's death was a beautiful one. He had Alzheimer's disease for more than ten years and it was impossible to know just how much conscious or cognitive awareness he possessed. And yet, there was one day when I went to visit him and something about him seemed very different. I asked what was going on and he said, "You really don't want to know." Somehow, I knew immediately that he was aware, or had decided, that he was nearing death.

We gathered as a family to spend several days together and with him. The night before he died, as the interval between each breath increased, we sat in a circle around his bed, told him how much we loved him, and sang some songs. I leaned over his bed, sang "Let Me Call You Sweetheart," and kissed him. As I did, he puckered his lips. He must have possessed some awareness of what was going on around him even though he died few hours later. Perhaps he heard and understood what we were saying. Fortunately he was not in pain and he slipped across that threshold peacefully. Our family had the great satisfaction of telling him he was loved and appreciated.

We think of dying as a medical event, and medical intervention is often called for. If there is pain, medication is certainly appropriate. Many of us desire the legal right to end our lives with a physician's assistance if we are terminally ill and the pain becomes unbearable, but such assistance is currently available in only a few states. We can arrange for hospice and palliative care, but dying frequently is a slow process. It is during this period of decline that the principles and practice of an end of life doula become so important. This care can employ guided imagery, or music, or the simple comfort of being held or touched to soothe a dying patient. Those close to the dying also need support.

Now in my early nineties and in excellent health, I do not feel that my death is imminent. However, we never know what lies ahead and I have a great curiosity about how my final demise might occur. Will it be cancer, stroke, heart disease, pneumonia, an accident, Alzheimer's? Or will I die from something more likely and mundane like a fall? Will I handle this final phase of my life with courage and grace? I do what I can to take care of myself by practicing yoga and attending fitness sessions. I walk carefully and hold on to railings. Despite these efforts, eventually my body will fail and I will make that journey into death. It is a natural process. It is part of living. I hope I have a gentle, beautiful death. I hope I will be surrounded by those I love and who love me.

DISRUPTION

APRIL 2020

Dealing with Covid-19

My granddaughter Carolyn recently sent me an article from the Harvard Business Review written by Scott Berinato titled "That Discomfort You're Feeling Is Grief." As several employees were feeling a sense of grief, apparently the HBR editorial staff decided to focus on content that might be helpful during this dreadful pandemic. Berinato interviewed David Kessler who is considered an expert on the topic. Kessler was co-author with Elisabeth Kübler-Ross on the book *On Grief and Grieving: Finding the Meaning of Grief through the Five Stages of Loss*. He has also written *Finding Meaning: The Sixth Stage of Grief*. Kessler's perspective reminds me of the familiar phrase from Abraham Maslow: *If all you have is a hammer, everything looks like a nail.* He manages to turn almost all emotions into some kind of grief. Wikipedia defines grief as "the response to loss, particularly to the loss of someone or something that has died, to which a bond or affection was formed." This makes sense to me and I take exception to much of what Kessler has to say.

In the interview with Berinato, Kessler talks about "anticipatory grief," which, he says, "is that feeling we get about what the future holds when we're uncertain." In my view, that is not grief, but anxiety, a totally different emotion. In fact, later on he states that "Unhealthy anticipatory grief is really anxiety…." He does not say what *healthy* anticipatory grief might be. To equate grief and anxiety is to diminish and mischaracterize the roles each emotion plays in our lives, especially during stressful times such as we are living through now.

In applying Kübler-Ross's stages of grief to the Covid-19 pandemic, Kessler says: "There's denial, which we say a lot of early on: *This virus won't affect us.* There's anger: *You're making me stay home and take away my activities.* There's bargaining: *Okay, if I social distance for two weeks everything will be better right?* There's sadness: *I don't know when this will end.* And finally there's acceptance. *This is happening; I have to figure out how to proceed.*" He goes on to say, "Acceptance, as you might imagine, is where the power lies. We find control in acceptance. *I can wash my hands. I can keep a safe distance. I can learn how to work virtually.*"

I do not find the stages of grief as a useful guide for understanding our reactions to the coronavirus. Though acceptance is an important quality to cultivate, I would not characterize it as giving us power by suggesting that we are in control. On the contrary, acceptance means that we realize we are not in control. By acknowledging what is happening and trying to figure out how to proceed, we are admitting that we are in the midst of a global pandemic that causes us enormous stress. There are things we can do, like washing our hands, wearing a mask, and keeping a safe distance, that help mitigate the situation, but we are not in control of its inevitable sweep or on how it will most certainly cause major disruptions in our daily lives. Struggling against the discomfort only causes us more suffering. We can find more strength, peace, and serenity if we cease resisting our very real concerns and accept the fact that our feelings of fear and anxiety are genuine. We have every reason to be deeply concerned about the rising numbers of coronavirus infections.

This current state of affairs is unlike anything I have experienced in my very long life. I was not prepared for such an upheaval and have been thrown into a state of confusion. Which experts should I believe? To what extent must I follow the recommendations for sheltering-in-place, or social distancing? How dangerous is it to be with others? How will I fill my time? How can I keep in touch with family and friends? What if I get sick? What if one of my family members gets sick? This highly contagious virus calls us to make decisions based on sometimes conflicting (and often false) information and asks us to adapt in unexpected and unfamiliar ways. I find these drastic changes to my habitual patterns of life both taxing and disorienting.

In this time of confusion and uncertainty, most of us experience a sense of unease, which can easily develop into anxiety. We worry because we have no idea when this pandemic will subside or when our lives will get back to some degree of normalcy. I have read (and agreed) that learning to live comfortably with uncertainty opens the door to all possibilities. But when we are in the midst of a pandemic, the future path of which is unknown, we are likely to feel more frightened than encouraged by those possibilities. In the meantime we must learn techniques that can distract us from worrisome thoughts. Breathing deeply and slowly for a few minutes or doing some exercises can be helpful in alleviating our apprehension. It is also important to get adequate sleep and to eat healthy food. We continue to hope that a treatment and/or vaccine is found so we can look forward to a more stable and sustainable world.

In discussing our emotional responses to the pandemic with a friend, she said that she is feeling "frustration, sadness, loneliness, boredom, appreciation of beauty, cynicism, and excitement." Her thoughtful list inspired me to think more about my own feelings, which are complicated, muddled, and mixed. Because this is such an extraordinary time, I am struggling to maintain a healthy equilibrium.

In addition to a general sense of disorientation and anxiety, I agree that frustration is one of the foremost effects. A "feeling of being upset or annoyed, especially because of inability to change or achieve something," aptly captures the sense of helplessness that overcomes us as we acknowledge that there is little we can do to help halt the spread of this virus other than comply, as best we can, with the guidelines offered by health experts. We are understandably annoyed because we are denied the usual freedom to move about freely and to gather in ways we are accustomed to. I am upset that I cannot have dinner out with my friends, or go to my yoga class or fitness session. I am especially distressed that our family gathering planned for this month had to be canceled.

Sadness is another feeling my friend and I share. An underlying heaviness is almost always present, something new for me. In the years before the onset of this global crisis I had attained a sense of contentment and serenity, especially in the last decade. I made new friends, found great fulfillment in my life and had created a routine that kept me both mentally and physically active—at least for someone my age. My sadness is unlike grief; it is a more generalized feeling, not specific to any particular loss but more pervasive. I am sad about the thousands of lives lost to this dreadful disease. I am sad about those who have lost their livelihood. I am sad I am not free to spend time with friends. I am sad that I cannot be with those I love who live far away. I realize there is a danger in allowing this sadness to deepen, for there is a possibility of spiraling into depression. All of us must guard against that.

Loneliness is yet another hazard of adhering to the rule of social or physical distancing. During my years of living alone I have found solitude to be suitable for my age and for my life style. It has given me more opportunity for contemplation, for self-discovery and self- realization, for getting in touch with my authentic self, a chance for what I have called the in-gathering of the soul's work. However, I am well aware that too much aloneness can be detrimental to our mental health. If we are not careful, we can become isolated, cut off from all human contact, which can bring on severe depression. In this era of social distancing we must be careful to maintain some kind of human interaction. I have found the use of phone calls or FaceTime to be enormously helpful in keeping in touch with my family and friends, thereby alleviating my loneliness.

Boredom is another peril in this time of being homebound. Many families have found innovative ways to help themselves and their children remain involved and active. One of my friends said that she, her husband, and two boys now plan and prepare each evening meal together. They also go for walks, play scrabble and other games. Jigsaw puzzles have become a welcome pastime for many people. Good books, and even those not so good, are a blessing. Netflix, Amazon, and other platforms provide an endless number of movies and series to watch. I have found, however, that it is best to avoid too much cable news; the shows are almost completely focused on the Coronavirus pandemic and much of it is disturbing. Watching in the late evening is not a way to get a peaceful night's sleep. I am trying to find satisfying ways to spend my time, such as staying in touch with friends, reading, and (of course) examining and attempting to clarify my thoughts in order to write these reflections.

Appreciation of beauty was a response that had not occurred to me until I realized that, although having fresh flowers in my house has always been important to me, having them around now is even more vital. Their beauty and color help brighten my spirit. We can walk or drive through our neighborhood or parks, marvel at the greenness of the budding trees, admire the brilliant, colorful tulips and be amazed by the vibrant redbud trees. I have also begun lighting candles. There is something about the soft, beautiful light of a candle that comforts me and somehow gives me hope that we can eventually return to a less restricted way of life.

My friend's list also included cynicism, a reaction that surprised me. Assuming cynicism refers to the belief that people are only interested in themselves and are not sincere, we only have to hear our president's comments to realize how exposed we all are to cynicism. Trump's inability to reach beyond his own self-interest, his total lack of empathy for those who have died or are suffering or are working to protect and serve others, and his daily spewing of lies are truly appalling. What we might focus on is how to avoid becoming cynical ourselves. It is vital that we continue believing in the goodness of people, doing whatever we can to help our democracy survive, and holding on to the hope that we will get through this period having become stronger. Reaching out to others to express our concern for their wellbeing instead of dwelling on our own distress is another way we can avoid becoming cynical.

While I am feeling apathy and lethargy, my friend's final word is excitement. This was puzzling to me, so I asked her to explain how she is experiencing excitement. She mentioned a number of very specific examples: listening to the Hallelujah Chorus on Easter morning; getting her stimulus money (which she shared with a friend); having a plumber easily fix her stopped-up sink. While I find it hard to work up much energy or enthusiasm for even the most mundane tasks, she is able to find excitement in small things. That perspective is very helpful, and I shall try to implement it in my own life. Mostly I sit like a lump, reading or staring out at my garden, which, oblivious of the death tolls that mount daily, is emerging into renewal—hostas, liriope, and other perennials springing up everywhere. That does provide me with joy and excitement. I shall try to remember those pleasures more often.

Kessler, who has named *meaning* as the sixth stage of grief, has said that he believes we find light in our darkest hours. But he does not tell us what meaning might be found in our current crisis other than connecting through our phones or going for walks. Surely there is more we can learn from this terrifying, insane time. I am searching to find for myself what that meaning might be. One of my good friends suggested that one lesson might be that "At a global level, perhaps Gaia is reminding us of our interconnection with the rest of the earth's species by showing us that we humans are not separate from each other and other species. The web of Indra is spinning before our eyes." He goes on to suggest another, that "On a national level I see the toxic effects of our myth of American exceptionalism, that we are blessed and better than other people."

While I admit to moments of near panic and despair, I wish to conclude with one final, uplifting sentiment that is important for us to keep in mind, and that is gratitude. I am thankful for, and in awe of, all those people I do not know, all those health care workers—doctors, nurses, ambulance drivers, and others who are attending the sick and dying—also the grocery clerks, the repair men, the bus drivers, the restaurants offering pick-up food—all those brave souls who are doing their best to keep our society functioning. On a more personal level, I am deeply grateful to my friends and family members who make the effort to pick up the phone, do FaceTime, send an email, or who are willing to risk a visit as we maintain our proper distance. It is our relationships and our interactions with those we love, even if virtual, that sustain us and help us through these challenging times.

MAY 2020

TRANSFORMATION

During this time of pandemic, many of us have been confined to our homes, describing this state like being in a cocoon. Actually, cocoons give way to moths and chrysalises house the larvae of butterflies. In either case, it is there where profound and mysterious transformations take place. A ravenous caterpillar, such as the one illustrated in the children's book "The Very Hungry Caterpillar," eats itself into a state of completion and corpulence, then builds itself a protective covering. After a period of time, the caterpillar (or what was once a caterpillar) breaks out of its confinement totally changed. It has become something completely, unrecognizably other than what it was.

Most of us tend to ignore or romanticize what happens inside those cocoons. We imagine the caterpillar, somehow magically growing colorful wings, then suddenly appearing as a glorious moth or butterfly fluttering through our gardens. But such is not the case; what does go on can only be characterized as gruesome. The caterpillar slowly devours itself until it has become a rather ghastly pile of amorphous gunk. Having almost entirely disintegrated, what remains are imaginal cells or discs. It is most intriguing that these cells are called "imaginal". It is as if the fundamental essence of the caterpillar has somehow provided a means by which a future butterfly might be imagined. These discs are the foundation of the new creature, the celebrated butterfly, which has matured as it fed itself off the residue of its antecedent, the caterpillar.

The example of the caterpillar and the butterfly is an extreme example of metamorphosis. There appears to be no relationship, certainly no outward resemblance, between the two, and yet we know they are merely different stages of development of one entity. In a sense, the caterpillar has paid a high price in the process of becoming a butterfly; it has basically disappeared, dissolved into a formless, gooey mess, no longer recognizable as the being it once was. But the transformation has given it an unexpected new freedom: now it has the ability to experience broadly expanded horizons. It can fly!

This biological happening can serve as a metaphor for our current situation. We are living through an unusual period of confinement. Undoubtedly these months of relative isolation will bring about significant changes within us. Though we certainly are not likely to disintegrate, it is quite possible that we will emerge considerably altered by the extraordinary circumstances of our current lives, perhaps hardly recognizable as our former selves. Due to the stresses of the quarantine, many of us have floundered, been frustrated, struggled with sadness or depression, more than once dissolved into tears, and have felt despondent in the face of imposed rules regarding our ability to come together. Some of us have had what we might call meltdowns. Like the caterpillar, we may be eating and drinking too much. We have, out of necessity, changed many of our habitual ways and will continue to change in ways both large and small. Some of us have been deprived of livelihoods; others, such as first responders, face terrible dangers every day, and still others have lost friends and family members to this deadly pandemic. Even if our personal lives have not been so drastically altered as some, nevertheless, our knowledge of these profound life experiences cannot help but alter how we think, how we live, and in how we view the world. We cannot possibly emerge from this unprecedented time untouched.

The question we might ask ourselves is whether we have the equivalent of imaginal cells. Do we possess the kind of fundamental beliefs and values that provide a solid framework that allows us to envision enhanced images of ourselves once we are able to free ourselves and resume a more normal way of life? At present we have no idea how long we must remain in our allegorical cocoons, nor do we know what our country and the world will be like once the pandemic has subsided. Let us hope, however, that as we are living through this period of crisis, we are transforming into more humane, compassionate, loving human beings. Let us attempt to grow metaphorical wings, which will enable us to move freely, using our newly transformed selves to bring beauty and kindness to the world around us.

JULY 2020
Living with Uncertainty

We are living in a time of great uncertainty. This disquieting period of our history is due to several distinct crises, none of which seems near resolution. Foremost is the global pandemic caused by Covid-19, a coronavirus. It originated in China in late 2019, and is believed to have been transmitted from bats to humans. Since it is new, scientists are scrambling to discover precisely how it is spread, which demographics are most vulnerable, which treatments may be effective, and how long those who have had the disease possess immunity. Symptoms vary from none to relatively mild to those requiring ventilators for months on end. Efforts at developing a vaccine have been accelerated, though estimates are that it will be 2021 before one is available.

Our government was made aware of the hazards of this highly contagious, lethal virus in January 2020, but failed to respond in a timely and aggressive way to stem the spread. As I write (July 2020), we are now the country with the most cases and with the most deaths from this deadly disease. We continue to receive conflicting information from our government regarding what guidelines to follow to protect our health. When and where are facial masks required? Under what conditions and how much distance must we keep between ourselves and others? When should we be tested for the virus and how can we arrange that? How careful should we be regarding human contact? Should schools be open, and if so, under what conditions? If we test positive but are not sick, are we still capable of transmitting the disease? (Indications are that both pre-symptomatic and asymptomatic individuals can spread the virus.) When, with the encouragement of our president, some states have opened public places despite the guidelines that have been issued by the CDC, this has usually been followed by a marked surge in the number of cases and hospitalizations. There is still much we do not know about this dangerous and bizarre coronavirus. It will take years of research before it is fully understood. In the meantime, we live with uncertainty.

As a result of the pandemic we are experiencing profound economic disruption with the possibility of economic collapse. We are told that the most effective way to control the spread of the virus is to avoid contact with others. This has meant the closing malls, restaurants, bars, offices, gyms, and any place where people are in close contact. Millions have been furloughed from their work, or have lost their jobs altogether. Some are fortunate to be able to work from home; others must work regardless of the risk to their health. Unemployment rates are the highest since the Great Depression. Though some financial aid has been provided, it is far from adequate to provide long term economic security. Evictions are growing since many families cannot afford to pay rent. Economic insecurity contributes to our sense of uncertainty.

Then, on May 25, a Black man, George Floyd, allegedly passed a counterfeit $20 bill at a neighborhood convenience store in Minneapolis. Police were called and following some initial interactions, Floyd was forced to lie face down on the pavement while a white police officer knelt with his knee on Floyd's neck for eight minutes and forty-five seconds (later found to be more than nine minutes.) A video of the event showed Floyd repeatedly complaining about not being able to breathe. Regardless, the officer kept his knee on Floyd's neck for two more minutes even after a fellow officer reported that he no longer could find a pulse. Floyd was declared dead when he arrived at a hospital. Officer Derek Chauvin has been charged with second degree murder.

This horrendous scene sparked a series of massive demonstrations throughout our country, continuing even to this day. Floyd's death was only one example of the overt racism displayed by many policemen against persons of color, some of whom are killed even though unarmed and nonthreatening. But the blatant, inexcusable murder of Floyd by white officer Chauvin unleashed an extraordinary outpouring of protests throughout our country. Unlike many previous demonstrations, these were populated by persons of all ages, all ethnicities, all colors. It has been estimated that as many as 15 to 26 million persons participated. The Black Lives Matter movement, begun in 2013, which advocates for non-violent civil disobedience in protest over police brutality against African-Americans, gained national and international attention during the weeks of protests. The organization also has advocated defunding the police, using those funds to invest in additional social services for Black communities.

These massive demonstrations seemed to awaken the awareness of the previously largely unacknowledged systemic racism in our country. The presence of numerous public statues of Confederate leaders, the display of Confederate flags, the names or mascots of sports teams using Native American imagery, have all come under attack in ways not previously thought possible. Though certainly not fully resolved, what to do with these examples of racist symbols and images is at least being discussed. It is yet to be seen if fundamental change will result from our still evolving understanding of the pain many of these monuments and names has caused African-Americans and Native Americans. While long overdue, it is another example of the uncertainty of our times.

Another crisis that has been with us for a while and which has been ignored for too long is climate change. It is widely accepted by scientists that the changes in the Earth's climate since the early 20th century have been caused largely by human activities, most especially by the use of fossil fuels. Burning these fossil fuels increases the levels of greenhouse gas in the Earth's atmosphere, raising the Earth's average temperature. In addition to warmer land temperatures, other indicators are warmer ocean temperatures, rising sea levels, ice loss at the poles and mountain glaciers, and the frequency and severity of extreme weather such as hurricanes, heatwaves, wildfires, droughts, floods, and precipitation.

There are several things we can do to mitigate climate change, mainly by reducing human emissions of greenhouse gases. Fossil fuels account for about 70% of these emissions, so we need to substitute low-carbon energy sources such as wind and solar power. Other ways to help would be reforestation and reducing energy demand by increasing energy efficiency. On a personal level, we can drive less, buy more efficient appliances, plant trees, or install solar panels on our homes. But perhaps the most obvious thing we can do to alleviate the inevitable effects of climate change is to vote for an administration that respects and utilizes the information that climate scientists can provide to help implement well-informed public policies. In the meantime, we are uncertain about how these inevitable changes in our weather patterns will affect our lives.

In anthropology liminality is defined as a period of ambiguity and disorientation that takes place in rites of passage. The term can also apply to periods of cultural and political change when established societal patterns are dissolved or upended. We are currently living through such a period of profound transition, with no clear indication of what might emerge after the confusion and chaos subside. Since many of the laws, customs, and conventions that have prevailed in the past have been abrogated by our current administration, we find ourselves in an indeterminate state. We are no longer the country we once were, but not yet the country we will become. We do not know what life will be like in two weeks, two months, or even two years. What new norms will be established depends in great measure on our election in November. It is essential that Trump be defeated.

Psychologically, uncertainty can be extremely unsettling. It can cause fear, despair, helplessness, and anxiety.

We worry about our health and that of those we love. We are upset about those without jobs or a place to live. We are alarmed about the persistent racism and the rising levels of violence. We fear for the future of our planet. Though these are legitimate concerns, it is also essential that we pay attention to our emotional state. If we are experiencing stress, discomfort, or pain, it is important to acknowledge those negative feelings but at the same time to attempt to maintain some sense of optimism.

Kristin Wong, in an article published in *The New York Times* on April 29, 2020, suggests a number of ways to be hopeful about the future, even when the future seems wholly negative. First is to practice self-compassion. It is often easy to be too hard on ourselves, but it is wise to remember that we are doing the best we can. If we fall into a pattern of self-blame, stop, breathe, think what we can do to protect ourselves, what would give us comfort and reassurance.

Another suggestion is to find pleasure in small things. Many people find walking to be helpful. I like sitting in my garden. Having a cup of tea or a glass of wine can be calming. Listening to music is often soothing. Reading a good book provides distraction from the news of the day. Playing cards or games can be fun. Some of us even like putting together a 5,000 piece puzzle!

Finding meaning is an important aspect of dealing with the stresses we are feeling. Perhaps it is a good time to re-read Victor Frankl's book *Man's Search for Meaning*. Finding ourselves deprived of our usual human contacts has helped many of us discover how vital those connections with family members and friends are to our lives. Though we cannot always interact in person, we can maintain contact by email, phone, FaceTime, or Zoom. These are not perfect solutions to our loneliness and social isolation, but they do help.

We cannot and should not deny the negative feelings that arise during this stressful, uncertain time. But we can learn to allow these disturbing moods to exist alongside our more positive attitudes. Resilience requires acknowledging and accepting our emotional complexity, understanding that we can be both disheartened and cheered at the same time. The ability to hold conflicting feelings in tension is an indication of emotional maturity. So, for myself and for all of you, as we live through this time of uncertainty, I suggest that we admit our occasional feelings of despair, but do not fail to resolutely hold on to hope!

JULY 2020

Reciprocity

During these times of social distancing and limited travel, I miss my usual interactions with friends and family. Our ability to make plans, to travel, to count on the routines of work and school have largely been upended by the bizarre and highly contagious coronavirus Covid-19. This adds to the stress of these uncertain times. My friend Sara and I spoke on the phone about these losses. She sent me this quote by Bessel van der Kolk, a psychiatrist who specializes in the area of post-traumatic stress. He is a professor of Psychiatry at Boston University School of Medicine and president of the Trauma Research Foundation in Brookline, Massachusetts. Though our symptoms may not qualify as clinical PTSD, nevertheless most of us are aware of changes, some subtle and some not so subtle, in our behavior and in our outlook. His words, especially his concept of reciprocity, resonate with me during this stressful time, so I felt moved to share them with you.

Social support is the most powerful protection against becoming overwhelmed by stress and trauma. ... The critical issue is reciprocity: being truly heard and seen by the people around us, feeling that we are held in someone else's mind and heart. For our physiology to calm down, heal, and grow we need a visceral feeling of safety. No doctor can write a prescription for friendship and love; these are complex and hard-earned capacities.

To Van der Kolk, reciprocity is "being truly heard and seen by the people around us, feeling that we are held in someone else's mind and heart." But he does not address the fundamental principle of reciprocity: if we are being truly heard and seen, we must, in turn, truly hear and see those with whom we are interacting. In order for reciprocity to take place there must be some kind of interaction or connection, either on a personal or on a societal level. Reciprocity requires a link or a situation that provides for the exchange of goods and/or services. The current demand for social distancing makes that more difficult to arrange, but is nevertheless crucial to our mental and communal health.

While van der Kolk addresses the personal or psychological importance for reciprocity, it is not a new principle. We see it first as far back as the 1700s BCE in Hammurabi's code, the familiar "eye for an eye" rule. If you break my arm, then I get to break yours. (Interestingly, the law allowed for only half payment if a man caused harm to an enslaved person.) The principle evolved and by the time of ancient Greece the mutual exchange of gifts was common. If an immediate exchange could not be arranged, then the practice of deferred reciprocity became accepted. The concept of a network of obligation, that is, an exchange of goods and services, has been beneficial to the growth and sustainability of cultures.

One obvious, simple example of reciprocity that we can now embrace is wearing face masks when in public places. If

I wear one, I am protecting you in case I might be an asymptomatic carrier of the virus. In the same manner, when you wear one, it is to protect me from possible infection. We are engaging in behavior that is easy and mutually respectful.

On a more personal level, studies have shown that when we offer support and kind words, our friends are much more likely to respond with similar friendly gestures. The opposite is likely true: if we are hostile to others, then they are more likely to be nasty to us. It is good to remember that kindness begets kindness. The essence of reciprocity is an acknowledgement and appreciation of our interdependence. Humans need human contact, and that contact involves an understanding of what it means to give and take. I give what I can, whether it is material goods (money), emotional support, or physical care, and the recipient in turn offers whatever he or she has in exchange; it need not be the exact same thing, but the sense of mutuality is maintained.

It occurred to me that reciprocity and symbiosis might be similar concepts. But such is not the case. Symbiosis is a biological term which refers to a close interaction between different biological organisms, such as parasites, or bacteria that live within our bodies. Reciprocity, on the other hand, is a social construct, which is determined by how humans and their communities respond to each other's needs and expectations. Reciprocity suggests a kind of moral obligation, and thereby contributes to the successful functioning of society.

These are the qualities that we value most in our partners and in our friends. I live alone, so having the opportunity to be heard and to be seen is critically important to my wellbeing. When I sit in my garden with my friends, or when I am able to be with family members, when I can both talk about my anxieties and listen to theirs, I feel bolstered, reassured, and comforted. True reciprocity requires that I provide them with the same attention and concern.

AUGUST 2020

Ennui and Angst

In the words of author Amor Towles, it is "that dreaded mire of human emotions." During this time of pandemic, social distancing, mask wearing, lockdown, online learning, and virtual gatherings by Zoom, many of us are suffering from *ennui*. This French word is defined as "a feeling of listlessness and dissatisfaction arising from a lack of occupation or excitement." It is often described as boredom, but what I feel is not boredom exactly, but rather a psychic weariness. It is not physical, though I do have a sense of heaviness around my shoulders. Lacking a daily requirement of productivity might explain my ennui, but some who are employed are also suffering from this dis-ease. I am not lacking excitement, since our daily news is filled with stories of protests, racial unrest, and rising numbers of virus cases and deaths. There is also the continuing chronicle of presidential incompetence and dishonesty. Nevertheless, I suffer almost daily from the weight of dullness and tedium which manifests as meaningless mental meandering, a frustrating incapacity to focus, and a relentless aimlessness. It is as if my life has lost some of its direction and much of its zest.

According to historians, the word *ennui* became popular during 18th century European romanticism when a writer suggested that ennui is "a fashionable kind of boredom brought on by weariness with the world," or "an attitude of lethargic disappointment, a preoccupation with the fundamental emptiness of existence." Perhaps emptiness does not accurately describe the mood currently affecting so many of us, though certainly there is a measure of lethargic disappointment, due in part to the futility of making long-range plans. We are suddenly aware that we are no longer in control of our future. Perhaps we never were, but at least we had the illusion that if in July or August we planned a gathering for September or October, or even December, chances are it would happen. The persistent, unnerving uncertainty is surely a major component of my disquiet.

Angst is another word that applies to our times. In German, Dutch, and Danish it means fear, and is akin to anguish, anxiety, and anger. One apt definition is "a feeling of deep anxiety or dread, typically an unfocused one about the human condition or the state of the world in general." I found a deeper understanding in the words of Danish philosopher Søren Kierkegaard. He described angst as "a type of anxiety that arises in response to nothing in particular, or the sense of nothingness itself. It's not exactly fear, and not the same as worry, but a simple fact of the human condition, a feeling that disrupts peace and contentment for no definable reason." Freud used the term for generalized anxiety. An element of suffering is also implied. However, rather than Kierkegaard's view that it arises "in response to nothing in particular," we have ample reasons for our feelings of angst. We are enduring a pandemic with all its health and economic consequences while also facing a cultural upheaval regarding the systemic racism that exists in our country. Each week brings new demonstrations caused by the shooting of an unarmed Black man by police. As if that is not enough, hurricanes and wildfires are devastating parts of our nation.

Though some of us worry more than others, one of the most obvious reasons for our angst is the fear of becoming ill with Covid-19 or of unknowingly transmitting it to others. Since the illness is highly contagious and can be spread even by those who are asymptomatic, we are told to maintain a distance from others and to wear a mask when in public places. We must constantly balance the risks of contagion with the need for shopping for necessities and for maintaining social contacts. Our angst moves to anger when we think about the mishandling of the pandemic in its earliest days. The loss of income, of homes, the economic ruin of many businesses large and small, all contribute to feelings bordering on despair. The suffering aspect of angst is especially prominent as we think of those who are ill and the hundreds of thousands who have died.

Our angst is further heightened by concerns regarding the coming election in November. Will it take place as scheduled, and if so, will it be conducted fairly? There are many signs of possible pending disruption, not least of which is major interference with the normal functioning of the United States Post Office. Will absentee ballots be delivered on time? With the appointment of a Trump flunky to run the postal service, there are good reasons to fear that might not happen. I fear that I do not have the stamina to stand for hours if there are long lines on November 3, so

I have arranged to vote early, in person. Defeating Trump and electing the Biden/Harris ticket is of utmost urgency so my fear that my ballot may not arrive in time to be counted creates further angst.

During stressful times we can expect to experience feelings of either ennui or angst—or perhaps both. What we need is an antidote to these negative mindsets, something that will contribute to a healthier mental state. One that comes to mind is *hope*. Hope that an effective vaccine will be developed. Hope for improved treatments for those ill with coronavirus. Hope that our election in November will restore the competency and constitutional values that are so essential for the survival of our democracy. In addition to hope is the importance of finding *joy*. If we can determine what delights us, however small and seemingly insignificant, then we can help mitigate those detrimental mental states that have been provoked by the troubling times in which we live.

The things that bring us joy are personal, so each of us must search for our own. Sitting in my garden alone, sometimes sipping a glass of wine, reflecting on my life and my relationships, engenders in me a tremendous sense of joy and serenity. The sound of the water burbling over the rocks into my small pond is soothing, as is the occasional resonant tones from my wind chime. The bells from a nearby church ring on the hour and half hour, gently reminding me of the passing of time. The shimmering leaves of the magnificent river birch which stands guard over my garden enchant me. The plants and flowers nourish me with their lushness. This morning I snipped a small branch of mint, and inhaling its pungent aroma infused me with a pleasurable sensuality. Recently I was thrilled when a hummingbird found its way to the red begonia hanging in my garden. Having friends join me in my sanctuary, exchanging stories and observations, discussing topics that engage and challenge my thinking, also gives me immense pleasure. Reading a good book sustains me. Watching an amusing Netflix series provides entertainment. All these bring me joy.

As we endure the inevitable acrimony and ugliness of this presidential election, ennui and angst will undoubtedly arise within us. My wish is that you, my family and friends, will help assuage those negative feelings by finding your own sources of joy. May they be plentiful.

JANUARY 2021

Our Unfinished Nation

The invasion of our nation's Capitol by a riotous mob on January 6 left me on edge, fearful of further violence as January 20, the day of our Presidential inauguration, approached. I had not been fully aware of just how much anxiety and tension I carried until tears of relief and release began to flow as Joseph R. Biden was sworn in as President alongside Kamala Harris as Vice-President. Thousands of troops and newly erected tall fences topped with barbed wire around an extended perimeter of the Capitol curbed the threat of violence. The optics were clearly different from what has been a routine ceremony that takes place every four years when a new administration takes office. This inauguration was like none other in our history. Our democracy was endangered not by foreign adversaries, but by home-grown domestic terrorists.

As many commentators have written, the incitement to insurrection by President Trump by encouraging his followers to storm the Capitol was shocking, but not surprising. He frequently recommended violent behavior against protestors or against the press, those that he held in contempt. But the viciousness, the extensive damage, the apparent effort to actually capture or kill members of Congress, including vice-president Pence, by some members of the mob was almost impossible to grasp. Fortunately all lawmakers were quickly led to secure locations. Unfortunately, five persons lost their lives during the wild attack. The president made no effort to stop the insurrection, but allegedly watched it unfold on TV, safely ensconced at the White House.

This outbreak of extreme hostility was due primarily to President Trump's refusal to admit that he lost the election held on November 3. After all the votes were counted, it became clear that Biden had prevailed by more than seven million votes and had won the Electoral College 306 to 232. After more than sixty courts had found no evidence of voter fraud, Trump and his followers continued to insist that he had won. He persisted in spreading outrageous conspiracy theories. A preponderance of Republicans refused to acknowledge the validated electoral votes for Biden and Harris even after the insurgence had taken place.

The final weeks of 2020 were extremely stressful for those of us who follow the political scene closely. The word *unprecedented* has been used repeatedly regarding the Trump presidency, and is entirely appropriate. To name just a few transgressions, he upended governmental norms, ignored established traditions, disregarded ethical standards, alienated allies, held the Constitution in contempt, undermined democratic institutions, sanctioned corrupt practices, mishandled the pandemic, and was motivated solely by his insatiable need for personal attention. His extreme narcissism and pathological lying have been demonstrated time after time. More than 30,000 falsehoods have been attributed to him over his presidency, nearly half of them during his last year in power. His role in inciting the insurrection led to a second impeachment, the only president to have been impeached twice.

But now we have a new president with a totally different governing philosophy and with a distinctly different personality. Whereas Trump was boorish and brash, Biden is mannerly and measured. Biden's principal message is his desire to unite our exceedingly polarized country due in large part to Trump's disorderly behavior and disruptive rhetoric. Trump was perhaps the most divisive president we have ever had. Though he is gone, many of his followers maintain their fallacious belief that the election was fraudulent, stolen from their favored candidate. Outlandish conspiracy theories continue to flourish. This makes restoring faith in our mainstream press, reestablishing the prevalence of truth over false and discredited claims, rebuilding confidence in the competency of government, and reasserting a sense of decency and dignity, major challenges for the new administration.

It is much too soon to have an adequate perspective on the nefarious influence Trump has had on our citizenry and on our democratic institutions. The frightening scene of a mob in our Capitol breaking down doors, smashing windows, and beating police officers, is too fresh to wholly comprehend and integrate into our collective psyche. We do not fully know how widespread and how organized white nationalism is in our country and how much danger domestic terrorism poses for our democracy. We do know that we barely escaped a coup and that the threat remains. There are still dangerous authoritarian elements within our country and even within Congress.

Like most of you, I was deeply impressed by the young poet Amanda Gorman as she read her poem *The Hill We Climb* at President Biden's inauguration. Her line *"Somehow we weathered and witnessed a nation that isn't broken, but simply unfinished"* provided me with a more encouraging assessment of our current state of affairs. Even though our democracy appeared perilously close to being broken, perhaps, as she suggests, it is rather undergoing a limited period of tribulation and turbulence, leading to the possibility of positive change. Again in Gorman's words, *"But while democracy can be periodically delayed, it can never be permanently defeated."* We must hold on to the faith that once the dangers are recognized, we will find ways to halt the delay and further strengthen our fundamental democratic values. We must remain vigilant, stay informed, continue to support justice for all, and guard against cynicism and despair.

Just as many of us have found that personal trials and troubles often help us grow in strength and resolve, perhaps it is also true of our country. That appears to be what Gorman is saying in these lines:

> *That even as we grieved, we grew.*
> *That even as we hurt, we hoped.*
> *That even as we tired, we tried.*
>
> *But one thing is certain.*
> *If we merge mercy with might, and might with right, then love becomes our legacy and change our children's birthright.*

EPILOGUE

Enduring and Evolving

When I started writing the essays in this book, about three years ago, I expected it would deal mostly with my personal journey as I grow deeper into old age. It opens with a reflection from a quarter century ago that addresses a yearning that I might realize my full potential by ultimately blossoming into an open-hearted, worthy human being. Based on that goal, I had planned to focus here on the concept of *completion* as it applies to this stage of my life. Many of these essays do, in fact, deal with my efforts in that regard.

In many ways I do feel complete: whole, all-embracing, fulfilled, grateful. *Whole* in that I have come to accept my flaws and failures as part of who I am, a perfectly imperfect human being. *Embracing* in that I acknowledge all of it: my depressions, disappointments, and sorrows, while also knowing contentment, accomplishment, and joy. *Fulfilled*, for in spite of never having lofty ambitions, I have achieved far more than I ever imagined possible—an enduring marriage, a loving family, satisfying creative endeavors, a PhD in my later years, and devoted friends. I am profoundly *grateful* for the opportunities life has given me.

However, I had no idea that major disruptions would take place in our country, especially those during 2020 and the early weeks of 2021, and what impact they would have on my life. So, in the later essays, the emphasis shifts to a broader concern regarding not just my personal situation but also the state of our country.

The devastating pandemic which continues to bring so much illness and death, the growing dangers to our globe caused by climate change, and the political chaos which has erupted in the past few years, have caused me to reconsider the idea of completion. Perhaps it has to do with scale. My life span is decidedly finite; I am nearing its predictable end. Since my personal strivings are largely past, possibly I can be thought of as reaching a kind of completion. In contrast, our country will conceivably endure for an unlimited time. What it will become in the years ahead remains uncertain and unknown. It is still evolving, changing, certainly not nearing completion. I quote again the inspiring and hopeful words of the young poet Amanda Gorman:

We will rebuild, reconcile, and recover.
And every known nook of our nation and every corner called our country, our people diverse and beautiful, will emerge battered and beautiful.

Acknowledgements

Putting together this second collection of personal reflections has been greatly satisfying largely because I had the expert help and support of Maggie Middeke and Harriet Blickenstaff. Maggie applied her outstanding book-designer skills and creative talents to this volume just as she did with the previous one, *Late-Life Reflections*. In addition to her choice of interesting fonts she created the charming drawings that adorn the pages. Harriet, my editor, offered corrections and suggestions, as well as arranging the essays into appropriate categories. Her willingness to engage in frequent, thought-provoking conversations often gave me further insights. I am deeply grateful to both for their contributions and for their friendship.